MARKETING INSIDE OUT

SRINIVASAN SIVA RAO

INDIA • SINGAPORE • MALAYSIA

Notion Press

No.8, 3rd Cross Street,
CIT Colony, Mylapore,
Chennai, Tamil Nadu – 600004

First Published by Notion Press 2020
Copyright © Srinivasan Siva Rao 2020
All Rights Reserved.

ISBN 978-1-64899-691-7

Contents

Preface

Every expert was once a novice. Every conglomerate was once a start-up.

Let me begin this book with an honest submission that I never aspired to become a marketing professional when I was studying my postgraduate degree at *XLRI School of Management, Jamshedpur.* I reluctantly took up the job offer at *Developer Group India Pvt Ltd (DGPIL)* to market its project. The project gave me the first field experience in marketing and the success of the project made me realize the power of marketing. Over the years, I refined my marketing skills through knowledge acquisition and practical experience. This gave me the confidence to venture into an entrepreneurial journey, which transformed my life for the better.

If my venture into marketing was unpredicted, so is this attempt at writing a book. Even in my wildest dream, I never thought of writing a book on marketing. The nationwide lockdown to mitigate COVID-19 presented an ample amount of time to write this book. I have tried my best to explain marketing in simple words. This book will be extremely valuable for knowledge-seeking students, marketing enthusiasts as well as for budding marketers and a useful companion for experienced marketers. I hope you will enjoy learning about marketing through this book.

I use this opportunity to thank my mom, sister, family, and friends, who have been my constant support and motivation in my entrepreneurial journey as well as for completing this book. My dad and mom were both perfectionists in their ways of life. I believe I had it in me and it was tapped at the right moment.

I express my heartfelt gratitude to my uncle *Mr. Narayanan Vittal Rao,* to my brother-in-law *Mr. Ravi Raghavendran,* to the Partners of Green Chilli Brands – *Mr. Brian Thomas* and *Mrs. Preethi Ramesh,* to my senior colleague *Mr. Sreedhar,* without whom I may not be what I'm today and where I'm today. I also thank each one of my peers and colleagues from whom I have gained immense knowledge in sales and marketing.

Last but significant, critics remain in everyone's life to challenge you and unnerve you with their criticism. You can decide to crib, ignore, and shun them. You can also decide to take criticisms constructively and work on them. I register a special thanks to one such person whose criticism gave the much-needed impetus to explore the unexplored side of mine. I dedicate this book to that special person.

Srinivasan Siva Rao

May 18, 2020, Chennai

Is Marketing Different from Advertising?

Most people believe marketing is advertising and advertising is marketing and interchangeably use. In reality, the scope of marketing is much wider and deeper than the scope of advertising. Advertising is just one aspect of marketing. Through advertising, entities reach out to the target consumer group to sell their products or services.

This brings up the question, *what is marketing?*

Marketing *for products or services* involves a series of steps in conducting the market research, segmenting the market to identify a target consumer group, understanding the need/want of the target consumer group, conceptualizing and designing products or services to meet the need/want of target consumer group, developing the pricing strategy to achieve business turnover goals, positioning the products or services to the target consumer group, disseminating information about the brand, unique selling proposition, value proposition of the products or services to the target consumer group through advertisements, giving several compelling reasons to the target consumer group to buy products or services, making consumers experience the value proposition, the brand promise and the brand attributes of the products or services, and converting them as loyal repeat buyers.

During the product or service conceptualization stage, entities must consider competitors' products or services and their offerings to the target consumer group. Entities must also consider other factors such as the behavioral psychology of the target consumer group for the products or services, the production strategies to provide variation in the products or services, the economics to forecast the demand for products or services, and the inventory management in the distribution network.

On the other hand, marketing *for a brand* involves creating a brand with a unique recognizable identity for the brand's products or services, communicating the brand's legacy and the brand's promise, creating a positive perception about the brand in the minds of the consumers, making consumers associate with the brand's products or services, and converting them as brand loyal over a period of time.

So, *how is marketing different from sales?*

Marketing and sales are two different functions but highly interconnected.

In marketing, entities attract buyers to sell their products or services primarily through advertising. In sales, entities appoint salespeople to aggressively pursue with buyers, through a strong sales pitch, to sell their products or services.

The sales team can gather vital information for marketers on how consumers perceive the brand and its products or services and if there is any gap in the product conceptualization or design and/or in the positioning strategies/pricing strategies/marketing communication.

Therefore, entities must have a cohesive marketing department and sales department, including that of the customer relationship department, for the seamless flow of information across departments.

The advent of advertising platforms and the power of the internet have changed the way brands advertise and approach the target consumer group. However, the basics of marketing are universal. It will remain the same despite any technological advances. Marketing concepts, frameworks, terminologies, mediums, strategies, and metrics keep evolving to remain relevant with time. It is, therefore, an absolute necessity for marketers to get a solid understanding of marketing concepts, frameworks, terminologies, mediums, strategies and metrics, and penchant to embrace the latest technologies for marketing.

In subsequent chapters, you will learn various marketing concepts, frameworks, terminologies, mediums, strategies, and metrics but in simple words.

Marketing Framework

SWOT ANALYSIS

It is widely believed that Albert S. Humphrey, a management consultant, invented the SWOT framework in the 1960s during a convention at Stanford Research Institute while analyzing the data of Fortune 500 companies to develop a long-term executable plan.

SWOT stands for Strengths, Weaknesses, Opportunities, and Threats. Strengths and weaknesses are internal factors of an entity while opportunities and threats are external factors for an entity. An entity carries out SWOT framework analysis periodically to understand how well it is placed vis-à-vis opportunities and threats posed by the industry competition and macro-environmental external factors.

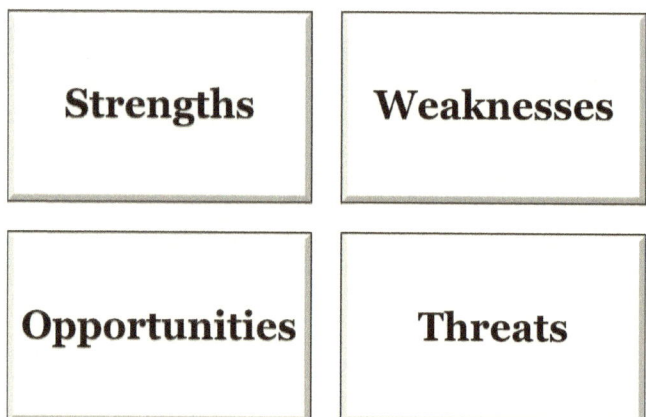

In the first step, an entity must list down all its Strengths, Weaknesses, Opportunities, and Threats.

An entity must compare its strengths and weaknesses with that of competitors on the following parameters – brand awareness, brand recall, brand recognition, brand legacy, brand promise, brand attributes, brand perception, brand association, brand loyalty quotient, brand value, unique selling proposition, value proposition, market share, production capacities, tangible assets, and intangible assets.

Compare opportunities and threats posed by existing industry competition, new entrants, substitutes, buyers' bargaining power, suppliers' bargaining power, political environment, economic outlook, socio-cultural values, technological advances, environmental challenges, and legal compliances.

In the next step, an entity must devise a strategy on the following:

1. How to maximize opportunities by leveraging strengths?
2. How to thwart or minimize threats by leveraging strengths?
3. How to minimize weaknesses by taking advantage of opportunities?
4. How to minimize exposure of weaknesses by avoiding threats?

PORTER'S FIVE FORCES

Michael E. Porter developed a simple framework in 1979, christened as *Porter's Five Forces*, to understand opportunities, threats, and competition level within an industry or a sector by analyzing an industry or a sector as a whole.

An entity carries out this framework exercise periodically to understand the market forces involved and recalibrate its marketing strategies so that the brand and its products or services remain relevant as well as competitive than that of its competitors.

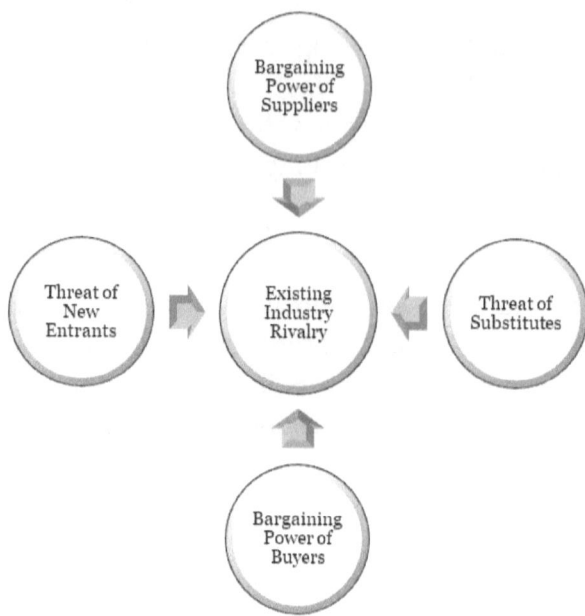

In **industry rivalry,** an entity analyzes the number of competitors in the market, brand awareness, brand recall, brand recognition, brand legacy, brand promise, brand attributes, brand perception, brand association, brand loyalty quotient, brand value, unique selling proposition, value proposition, market share, production capacities, tangible assets, intangible assets, positioning strategies, pricing strategies, pre-sales and post-sales services of each of the competitors vis-à-vis its offering.

In the **bargaining power of suppliers,** an entity analyzes the number of suppliers, the competitiveness of suppliers in terms of their production capacities, distribution network, and quality of raw materials. Less number of suppliers can put entities on the back foot as suppliers can drive input raw material cost. It might also be a scenario where there are many suppliers, but an entity cannot switch to other suppliers due to their low production capacities, inferior raw material quality, or poor distribution network. In such a case, only a few suppliers qualify to supply raw materials and they get the upper hand to dictate terms for an entity.

In the **bargaining power of buyers,** an entity analyzes the number of buyers, the significance of each buyer in terms of business revenues, the brand loyalty quotient, and the cost of switching to products or services of competitors/substitutes. If there are many buyers but a few accounts for large business turnover, then those few buyers command higher bargaining power. Similarly, if the competitors' products or services are priced competitively with almost the same brand attributes, brand promise, unique selling proposition, and/or value proposition, then buyers can switch to competitors easily. In such a case, an entity is on the back foot as it can hardly bargain with the buyers.

In the **threat of new entrants,** an entity analyzes entry and exit barriers for new entrants in terms of time, money, technologies, and regulations to establish in the market. In some sectors, entry barriers are minimal but exit barriers are significant. In some sectors, entry barriers are significant but exit barriers are minimal. In some sectors, entry and exit barriers are both minimal or both significant.

High-Entry High-Exit Barrier Sectors: In these sectors, the government frames acts, rules & regulations with the stringent entry and exit barriers, and completely controls the sector as it involves public interest and/or strategic interest. *Some of the examples of high entry and high exit barrier sectors are BFSI, Telecom, Oil & Gas, Nuclear, and Defense sectors.*

High-Entry Low-Exit Barrier Sectors: In these sectors, the government frames acts, rules & regulations to evaluate, qualify, and give consent to entities to run the business. But the government shall not place stringent exit barriers if entities decide to exit the business. *Some of the examples of high entry but low exit barrier sectors are Hospitals, Schools, Universities, and eCommerce sectors.*

Low-Entry High-Exit Barrier Sectors: In these sectors, investments made in the tangible assets and technologies can make the entities difficult to sell or relocate or write-off or exit the business. *Some of the examples of low entry but high exit barrier sectors are Luxury Hotels, Automobiles, Airlines, Wind & Solar Farm sectors, and IT/ITeS Companies in Special Economic Zones.*

Low-Entry Low-Exit Barrier Sectors: In these sectors, the government will not place too many stringent barriers for the opening and closing of businesses. A government might frame some acts, rules & regulations for public safety, unfair competition but they are not aimed at regulating the entry and exit of the businesses. *Some of the examples of low entry and low exit barrier sectors are Cab Aggregators, Hotel Aggregators, Standalone Retail Shops, and Standalone Restaurants.*

Governments across the world regulate barriers for entry and exit from time-to-time depending on the state of affairs, thereby making entry and/or exit easy or tougher. At times, the timing of entry into a sector itself creates a high entry barrier when the competition is intense or when the market is consolidated. At times, *people, money, tangible assets, intangible assets, brand loyalty, and technological know-how* act as entry and exit barriers for businesses.

In the **threat of substitutes,** an entity analyzes possible substitutes for a brand's products or services such as the number of substitutes available in the market, consumers' propensity for the substitutes, the cost, its availability, the ease of substitution and the closeness of substitute that can affect sales volume as well as business turnover significantly.

Quiz:

1. *Why has the Government of India created entry barriers for eCommerce companies when they are not of any public safety or strategic safety concern?*
2. *Why do wind and solar farms, IT/ITeS companies in special economic zones have high exit barriers?*
3. *What was the biggest barrier to the digital payment system in India? How has the Government of India eased technological barriers to usher in the era of the digital payment system in India?*

PESTEL ANALYSIS

Harvard Professor Francis J. Aguilar first introduced the term ETPS in his publication *"Scanning the Business Environment"* in the year 1967. The term was amended as PEST, which stands for Political, Economic,

Social-Cultural, and Technological. Later, Environmental and Legal factors were added to expand PEST as PESTEL.

PESTEL framework analyzes opportunities and threats posed by macro-environmental factors that can affect the industry or a sector as a whole and more so the entry, survival, and profitability of an entity.

Political factors that can affect the industry or a sector due to government policies and legislation are *tax laws, labor laws, trade restrictions, tariff restrictions, political stability, and policy changes.*

Economic factors that can affect the industry or a sector are *sectoral growth outlook, demand forecast, currency exchange rates, credit availability, bank lending rates, and inflation rates.*

Socio-cultural factors that can affect the industry or a sector are *age distribution, gender distribution, cultural difference, lifestyle variation, historical values, work ethics, and work attitude.*

Technological factors that can affect the industry or a sector are *R&D innovation, technology adoption rates, and workplace automation.*

Environmental factors that can affect the industry or a sector are *weather, weather changes, climate, climatic changes, earthquakes, floods, tsunami, and hurricanes.*

Legal factors that can affect the industry or a sector are *compliance cost to consumer laws, discrimination laws, copyright infringement laws, anti-trust laws, privacy laws, trade regulations, health and safety regulations, and environmental laws.*

ANSOFF MATRIX

Igor H. Ansoff published the Ansoff Matrix, *also called a* **Product/ Market Expansion Matrix,** in the Harvard Business Review in an article titled *"Strategies for Diversification"* in 1957. The Ansoff Matrix guides marketers and business owners to devise marketing strategies for further growth.

In the **market penetration strategy,** an entity organically grows to increase its market share by selling more units of existing products or services to existing consumers or by identifying new consumers for the existing products or services in the existing geographical market. It can inorganically grow by acquiring or merging or partnering with direct competitors to increase the market share.

Organic growth of increasing market share is by *increasing promotions, reducing prices, giving discounts, and strengthening distribution network.*

An example of organic market penetration by asking existing consumers to consume more in the existing geographical market: A wheat flour brand reduced its prices by 20% expecting its consumers to consume more quantities in a month.

An example of organic market penetration by identifying new consumers with existing products or services in the existing geographical market: A wheat flour brand intends to increase its market share by vociferously advertising that "wheat flour is good for diabetics and heart" and asking the target consumer group to give up on their rice intake and eat more of wheat flour.

An example of inorganic market penetration by acquiring a competitor brand: An online apparel brand acquires another online apparel brand offering apparel to the same segment in the existing geographical market to gain market share inorganically.

In the **market development strategy,** an entity organically grows by launching its existing products or services to new consumers in the new geographical market, or inorganically grows by acquiring or partnering with another entity selling similar products or services in the new geographical market.

If any entity wants to grow organically, then it must carry out marketing frameworks to understand opportunities and threats posed in the new geographical market and identify and understand the need/want of the target consumer group before entering into the new geographical market.

If any entity wants to grow inorganically, then it must check for synergies in business operations before acquiring or partnering with another entity.

In the **product development strategy,** an entity intends to introduce new products or services in the existing geographical market or tweaks its existing products or services to position it differently in the existing geographical market.

For introducing a new line of products or services in the existing geographical market, an entity carries out detailed market research to understand the gap between the demand of consumers and its line of product or service offerings to conceptualize, design as well as manufacture to sell new products or services.

An example of a product development strategy to organically grow by having new products or services in the existing geographical market: An FMCG company selling herbal hair oil identifies the demand for herbal hair cream and introduces a herbal hair cream product in the market.

Sometimes, an entity tweaks its existing products or services considerably for a different consumer segment in the existing geographical market. While doing so, an entity must take care not to cannibalize its existing products or services. This can be achieved by differentiating products or services to consumers through positioning, pricing, and value proposition.

An example of a product development strategy to organically grow by tweaking its products or services in the existing geographical market: An entity that is selling premium villas plans to introduce affordable villas by considerably lowering its specification to make villas affordable in the existing geographical market. Any misadventure to position affordable villas as premium villas can lead to the cannibalization of its premium villas. People might buy affordable villas instead of premium villas, only to get disappointed later due to lower specifications.

At times, an entity considers creating a new line of products or services as time-consuming and resource-consuming. Therefore, it acquires another entity, which is not a direct competitor in its business, to inorganically grow, provide synergies to its business and offer a better experience to consumers.

An example of a product development strategy to inorganically grow by acquisition in the existing geographical market: An FMCG company selling chemical-based products acquires an FMCG company selling herbal products in the existing geographical market.

In the **diversification strategy,** an entity intends to launch a new line of products or services to new consumers in the new geographical market.

The diversification strategies are a riskier option where an entity tries to grow its business turnover by venturing into unchartered territory where it requires both product development and market development. Though riskier, diversification strategies can be rewarding at times as it spreads the risk and ensures business continuity.

Diversification is of two types: *related diversification* and *unrelated diversification.*

In **related diversification,** there is a relationship between the entities and product/market matrix. Here entities venture into the new geographical market, organically or inorganically, where they can find a strategic fit through manufacturing synergies, operational synergies, technological synergies, supply-chain synergies, or cost-saving synergies.

A laptop manufacturing entity in a country starts mobile phone manufacturing in another country. Here, an entity can derive positive synergies with its manufacturing experience.

A boiler servicing company in a country starts servicing transformers in another country. Here, an entity can derive positive synergies with its operational experience.

An eCommerce industry in a country acquires a payment gateway company based out of another country. Here, an entity can derive positive synergies with technology.

A crude oil exporting entity in a country acquires a cargo shipment company based out of another country. Here, an entity can derive positive synergies through supply-chain.

An EPC entity in a country acquires a cement plant in another country. Here, an entity can derive positive synergies by cost-saving.

In **unrelated diversification,** there is no relationship between entities and product/market matrix. Here entities venture into any unrelated businesses in any geographic market where they find it profitable. Such entities are termed as *conglomerates.*

For example, a car manufacturing entity in a country acquires a tea brand in another country. The consumer base market for both products is completely unrelated. There can be no synergies between the two, but the entity might have researched business viability and profitability before the acquisition.

Quiz:

Mention the marketing strategy for the following:

1. *Ola expanding cab operations in India*
2. *Zomato's acquisition of Uber Eats in India*
3. *Uber's entry into the Indian mobility market*
4. *Walmart's acquisition of Flipkart*
5. *Ola Cabs launching Ola Money*
6. *Flipkart's acquisition of PhonePe*
7. *Microsoft's acquisition of Nokia Mobiles*

BCG MATRIX

Bruce D. Henderson, the founder of Boston Consulting Group developed the BCG matrix, *also known as* the **Growth-Share Matrix,** in 1968, to correlate market attractiveness and industry growth attractiveness to suggest further investment strategies.

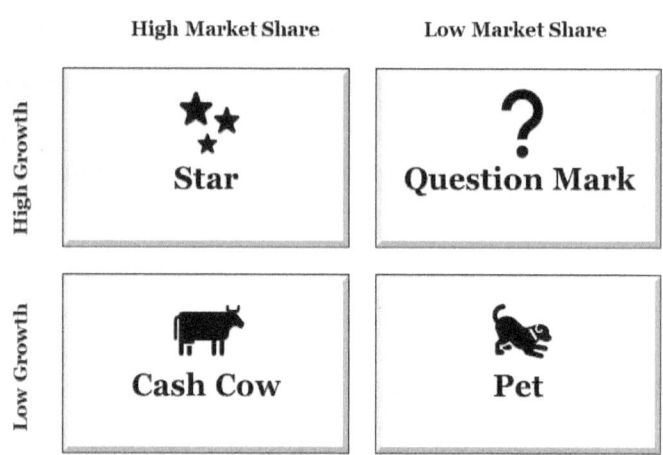

When an industry is in a nascent growing phase or when the industry has huge growth potential in the immediate future, an entity enters into a market and tries to increase its market share. More cash is pumped into the business to increase market share so that a *"question mark"* becomes a *"star"* and later becomes a "cash cow" as the industry matures and consolidates. An entity must periodically assess the market penetration and if it is unable to capture significant market share, then it must quickly decide whether to keep investing or exit the business to avoid any further bleeding of cash.

When an industry is fast-growing, an entity that has a high market share must invest to maintain market share, capture more market share, and fend-off competition. The high market share generates more cash, but the growth-phase of the industry consumes equally more cash until the industry matures and consolidates. This is the "star" phase in growth. Many entities get acquired or merged or even chucked out of the business.

Once an industry matures and consolidates, a "star" becomes a "cash cow" for an entity. When an industry matures, the growth slows down. In such a matured slow-growing industry, an entity that has a high market share typically generates more cash out of the business than the cash required to maintaining the business. Such entities should not invest more than required to maintain the business. Instead, these entities must milk "cash cows" to the extent possible to generate more cash to invest in innovating new products or services (product development), invest in a new market (market development), or diversify their businesses.

Despite injecting cash in several tranches, if an entity captures only a low market share, a *"question mark"* becomes a *"pet"* as the industry matures and consolidates. The entity generates just sufficient cash or sometimes negative cash returns due to a low-market share in a slow-growing consolidated industry. Under such circumstances, the entity must decide on continuing the business with a view to sell or liquidate or reposition the business.

Quiz:

1. *Analyze and articulate how market consolidation took shape in the Indian mobile telecom sector. Name the players who were cash cows, stars, question marks, and pets when the industry was consolidating.*

The 4Ps and Expanded 7Ps of Marketing Mix

The contemporary marketing mix – the 4Ps, was framed by E. Jerome McCarthy in 1960. However, it was Phillip Kotler, widely regarded as *the Father of Modern Marketing*, who popularised this 4Ps approach.

The contemporary 4Ps of Marketing Mix are *Product, Price, Promotion,* and *Place*. Marketers in the service industry also consider *People, Processes,* and *Physical Evidence* to make 7Ps of Marketing Mix.

Product: It refers to products or services that an entity intends to sell to its target consumer group. The product must fulfill the demands of the target consumer group. The target consumer group must at least believe that they want/need the product and the product will meet the demand of the group. An entity must decide on the *product design, product features, product quality, branding, unique selling proposition, value proposition, packaging, labeling, warranties, product guarantees, replacement guarantees,* and *money-back guarantees* vis-à-vis that of competitors' offering.

Place: It refers to where and how an entity intends to sell products or services to the target consumer group. An entity must decide on *the manufacturing base, geographic market, inventory management, distribution network, transportation, warehousing,* and *retailing*. It must also decide whether to sell through *physical brick-and-mortar stores or online stores such as through websites, apps, or any digital platforms*. An entity must also decide whether to sell through *channel partners, exclusive rights, selective rights, geographic rights, non-exclusive rights,* or *franchisee rights*.

Price: It refers to the price that consumers are paying or willing to pay. An entity must consider *the actual cost price, the sale price, the perceived value of products or services, the stage of product diffusion curve, promotional offers, discounts, cash backs, sale commissions, credit policy,* and *payment terms* vis-à-vis that of competitors' offering.

Promotion: It refers to *the promotion mix of the advertising (ad) platforms, the timing of ads, frequency of ads, the time gap between ads to reach the target consumer group through paid advertising, direct marketing, public relations, word-of-mouth,* and *referral marketing.*

In simple words, the marketing mix should aim at **promoting the right product in the right place at the right time with the right price.**

People: An entity must engage with the right people to manage the business affairs for delivering a full-value proposition to consumers. This includes identifying *investors, employees, service consultants,* and *material suppliers,* whose value and culture must orient that of the entity's values and culture.

Processes: An entity must develop processes and policies for *hiring, skill development, quality assurance, safety, buying cycle,* and *customer service* to ensure that a brand remains competitive and relevant to the changing times as well as the competition. These processes and policies must create a positive perception of the brand in the minds of the consumers.

Physical Evidence: As there are no physical attributes for services, which are intangible, an entity develops physical evidence where consumers can interact, experience, and get pleased with the services. The physical evidence can be an impressive *brochure, visiting card, corporate website, social media accounts or memorabilia, any hardcopy or softcopy material* that consumers can relate to.

Some marketers also consider **Performance** or **Productivity** thereby making it as 8Ps of Marketing Mix.

The Difference – Need, Want, Wish, Desire

Marketers must understand the difference between the need, the want, the wish, and the desire to position as well as communicate their products or services effectively to the target consumer group.

The need is an immediate and essential requirement of a person. Humans cannot survive if the need is not fulfilled. Non-fulfillment of the need leads to ill-health and even death. The need does not differ from person to person and does not change with time.

The need for *food, water, air, home, sleep, cloth, health,* and *peace* is essential as well as a universal requirement. Non-fulfillment of the need puts a question mark on human survival and human well-being.

On the other hand, the want is a non-essential wish or desire of a person. Humans can survive even if the want is not fulfilled. Non-fulfillment of the want leads to disappointment. The want differs from person to person and changes with time.

So, *is there any difference between a wish and a desire?*

A desire is a stronger form of a want. A person desires when he/she is adamant about his/her want and is capable of buying or confident of achieving, either now or in the future. Whereas, a wish is a lighter form of a want. A person craves when he/she is incapable of buying or not confident of achieving, either now or in the future.

Consider the following examples:

1. *I wish I could buy a Ferrari car in my life.*
2. *I desire to buy a Ferrari car.*
3. *I am buying a Ferrari car next month.*

In the first example, one wishes to buy a Ferrari car, but it looks like a distant, near-impossible dream for him/her. In the second example, one exhibits the desire to buy a Ferrari car but there is no intent expressed. In the third example, one exhibits the desire and intent to buy a Ferrari car in the next month.

Maslow's Hierarchy of Needs

The need/want is the base for a sale. Abraham Maslow categorizes "the need" into five types in his theory and puts them in a pyramid structure. Marketers must understand where their products or services lie in the hierarchy of needs, how their products or services will fulfill "the needs or the wants" of the target consumer group, and devise positioning strategies, pricing strategies as well as promotional strategies to convince people to buy their products or services.

Self
Actualization
Needs

Egoistic & Esteem
Needs

Social Needs

Safety Needs

Physiological Needs

Physiological needs are the internal, physical, and chemical requirements without which it becomes difficult for humans to survive. These are *food, water, air, basic clothing, basic shelter, sleep,* and *basic health.* Physiological needs are a universal need for humans to lead a stable life. Therefore, before aspiring for any other needs, humans pursue to satisfy physiological needs.

Once physiological needs are fulfilled, humans pursue to safeguard their self-interest and the surrounding environment. These are *physical security, economic security, emotional security, health,* and *well-being.* If humans do not feel safe, they do not think beyond safety needs.

Once basic physiological needs and safety needs are fulfilled, humans think of social needs. Humans want to love and be loved by others. They seek belongingness and acceptance by social groups – *families, friends, colleagues, mentors,* and *confidants,* be it small or large. Acceptance by social groups enhances their health and psychological well-being whereas rejection and isolation by social groups severely impact their health and psychological well-being.

When humans are satisfied with social needs, they seek to fulfill egoistic and esteem needs. The egoistic needs are feeling valued by others – *status, prestige, recognition, importance,* and *respect from others.* The esteem needs are feeling good about self – *confidence, inner-strength, talent, skill, ability, self-respect, self-esteem,* and *independence.*

When physiological needs, safety needs, social needs, and esteem/egoistic needs are met, humans pursue self-actualization. Here, contrary to the popular perception, self-actualization needs do not refer to detaching from the materialistic life. Rather it refers to pursuing larger goals. Self-actualized individuals realize that they are doing what they are meant to do in their life. They pursue to become the best in their field of work by *acceptance of facts, absence of prejudice,* and *realizing one's full potential.* But not every human set the same level of goals. Therefore, the self-actualization type and accomplishment level vary from person to person.

Quiz:

1. *Opting for a life cover insurance fulfils _____ needs.*
2. *Banks offering a personalized banker to an account holder fulfills _____ needs.*

Types of Market Research

Before launching new products or services, or before entering into a new market, entities conduct market research to understand the gap in the market and the demand of consumers. Market research is of two types: *primary market research* and *secondary market research.*

SECONDARY MARKET RESEARCH

Entities carry out secondary market research, before performing primary market research, to get first-hand business viability and understanding of the market.

This market research is relatively easy and cost-effective as this is carried out by extracting data from different sources, say *a government portal* or *a nodal agency* or *a previously conducted survey* or *a competitor's data,* and analyzing the data in the office rooms. This market research does not involve interacting with the target consumer group.

PRIMARY MARKET RESEARCH

Primary market research involves gathering fresh data through *a field survey, email/telephonic survey,* or *through web/social media platforms,* and then analyzing the data.

Though laborious and costly, this market research provides an exceptionally good understanding of the market.

> **Products or services that do not meet the demands of the consumers are doomed to fail.**

Which one is better?

Each market research has advantages and disadvantages. The accuracy of secondary market research depends on the availability, authenticity, sufficiency, validity, and relevance of the data of the desired target consumer group. In the absence of such data, entities must conduct primary market research without making any compromises.

Quiz:

1. *Brand X is planning to enter into a new market where Brand Z already exists. Brand X manufactures products that are similar to Brand Z. What market research will Brand X have to deploy?*
2. *Brand Y is planning to enter a new market where Brand Z already exists. Brand Y manufactures niche products that are not in the market. What market research will Brand Y have to deploy?*

Segmentation, Targeting, Positioning

Entities carry out segmentation to segregate the data obtained from the market research – based on *demographics, geography, interests, behaviors, values,* and *beliefs* – to get a meaningful insight into the data.

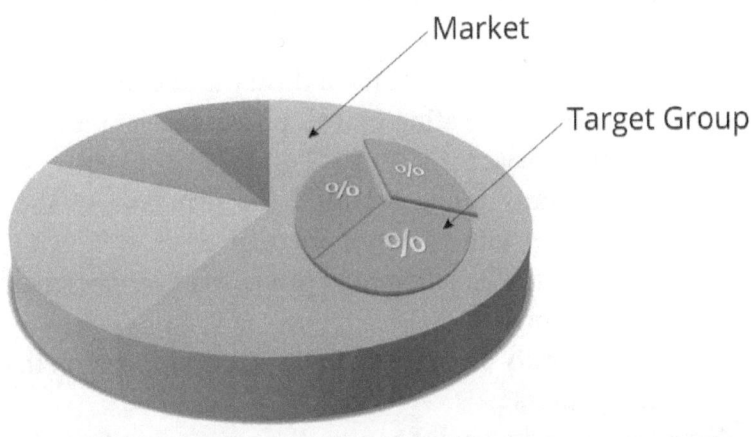

Once the segmentation step is completed, entities zero-in on a target consumer group within the market where they find demand, business viability & profitability to conceptualize, design, manufacture, and sell products or services. Some entities opt to produce generic products or services while some entities opt to produce niche products or services.

Segmentation and targeting help entities in doing away with some of the competitors in the market who are focused on the other segments and/or other target consumer groups.

Once the target consumer group is identified, entities focus on positioning products or services to create a positive perception of the brand in the minds of consumers by differentiating a brand's products or services from those of its competitors.

Entities carefully evaluate the following questions:

- What is the demand of the target consumer group?
- How big is the target consumer group in the market?
- Who are the competitors for the target consumer group in the market?
- Are there products or services meeting the demand of the target consumer group?
- How intense is the competition for the target consumer group in the market?
- What is the growth state of the industry in the market – nascent growth phase, accelerating growth phase, decelerating phase, or consolidation phase?
- How is an entity going to fulfill the demands of the target consumer group with its line of offering?
- How can an entity be different in products or services than those of its competitors?
- How can an entity be different in the value proposition than that of its competitors?
- How can an entity be different in the positioning than that of its competitors?
- How can an entity be different in the pricing strategy than that of its competitors?
- How can an entity be different in the promotion strategy than that of its competitors?

Quiz:

1. *A brand intends to sell beauty products for women. Who is the target consumer group? How will the brand go about segmentation, targeting, and positioning of its products?*
2. *A brand is selling basmati rice produced through inorganic farming methods and organic farming methods. How will the brand position the products in the market?*

Brand & Branding

The market is flooded with products or services. Consumers are bombarded with advertisements. This makes life difficult for entities to reach the target consumer group. Consumers also find it difficult to identify the best products or services in the market that meet their needs/wants.

Therefore, it is an absolute necessity for an entity to position its products or services by creating a brand, giving a brand identity, leveraging advertising platforms to create brand awareness, brand recall, brand recognition, to convey brand legacy, brand promise, brand attributes, brand value, unique selling proposition, value proposition through marketing communication, and to make consumers positively perceive the brand to carve out a strong customer base.

> *It takes years to build a brand and minutes to destroy!*

So, *why and how do we create a brand?*

A **brand** gives an assurance to its consumers that products or services shall meet consumers' expectations and shall be consistent in quality and performance at all times across all geographies. A brand is created by giving a brand identity to products or services with a brand promise statement.

A **brand identity** is given to products or services through a mix of *recognizable name, symbol, logo, tagline, shape, color, aroma, taste, jingles,* and *even a brand ambassador* to help consumers easily recognize, distinguish, and associate with the brand.

A **brand promise** is a bold statement made by an entity to its consumers about what it stands for and what consumers can experience through its products or services.

Therefore, **Branding** is the process of creating a connection between the brand and the consumers' functional, rational, and emotional perception of the brand.

When consumers experience quality or a feature that is inherent to the products or services, they attribute it to the brand itself. This is called **brand attributes.** *For example, authenticity, consistency, credibility, uniqueness, quality, performance, satisfaction,* and *customer service.* When consumers consistently experience these brand attributes, they perceive brands positively. A brand can leverage these brand attributes as a brand promise while launching new products or services, or when entering into new markets.

Creating **brand awareness** is by disseminating information about the brand through advertisements to the minds of consumers and making them aware of the brand through brand identity, brand legacy, brand promise, brand attributes, unique selling proposition, and value proposition.

When consumers are asked *impromptu* to name brands that sell particular products or services, they can typically recollect three to seven brands from their memory. This is called **brand recall,** which is an *unaided* or *a spontaneous recall.*

The very first brand that a consumer can recall from memory is the brand that has **top-of-the-mind-awareness** (TOMA), which greatly influences the purchasing behavior of the consumers.

When a consumer cannot recall a brand from memory but can recognize a brand with its brand identity, brand promise, brand attributes, or brand ambassador, it is called **brand recognition.** This is an *aided recall.* A brand imposes its brand identity, brand promise, brand attributes, or brand ambassador firmly in the minds of consumers so that consumers can quickly recognize and associate with the brand through sensory receptors – *visualization, smelling, tasting, hearing,* and *feeling.*

Some consumers expect the brand to be visibly noticed – *seeing repeat advertisements, seeing advertisements across various advertising platforms, being available in the store, being used by consumers in the market,* and *consumers vouching for the brand.* Therefore, **brand visibility** is being visible where the consumers are. Brand visibility increases the inner promise and belief of consumers that the brand is the right choice.

A piece of music can be noise to others.

People perceive a brand in different ways. **Brand perception** is how a buyer is looking at a brand rather than how a brand wants a buyer to look at it. Therefore, *brand legacy, brand promise, brand attributes, brand value, tangible performance, intangible experience, word-of-mouth, social reputation,* and *customer service* play a crucial factor in creating a perception for a brand.

When products or services meet or exceed the demand of the consumers, they develop a positive perception of the brand. As consumers continue to experience satisfaction on repeat purchases, they start associating with the brand and develop an emotional connection with the brand.

When products or services fail to meet the demand of consumers, *either due to unfair expectations from consumers or due to excessive promises by the brands to consumers,* they develop a negative perception of a brand.

Also, when a brand legacy and/or brand promise is compromised, or when society perceives a brand to be negative, consumers develop a negative perception of the brand. A negative perception severely affects the brand association.

Therefore, **brand affinity** is an emotional connection that consumers make with the brand. As consumers continue to experience the value proposition, they perceive the brand positively and this positive perception makes them brand loyal over some time.

Brand association is based on the positive attributes and perception of a brand that strikes the mind of the consumers when asked for. If they perceive the brand to be positive, they associate with the brand. If they perceive the brand to be negative, they dissociate from the brand.

Brand loyalty happens when one associates with the brand for a longer period. Brand loyalty helps an entity to lower marketing efforts and aggressive sales pitch. Over a period, this brand loyalty turns to **brand advocacy,** where brand loyal consumers start advocating for the brand through word-of-mouth in the market.

To check satisfaction levels and brand loyalty quotient, entities conduct the Customer Satisfaction (C-SAT) survey and the Net Promoter Score (NPS) survey. C-SAT surveys are to check on the short-term satisfaction levels on issues or complaints raised. In the C-SAT survey, consumers are asked to rate only one question on a scale of 1 to 5. On the other hand, NPS surveys are to check on the long-term satisfaction levels of the brand promises, brand perception, purchasing behavior, brand association, brand loyalty, and brand advocacy vis-à-vis that of its competitors. In the NPS survey, consumers are asked to rate a series of questions with different evaluating parameters and varying score patterns. Therefore, NPS surveys are generally longer and time-consuming for consumers to complete. Poor completion response is also an indicator of lower brand loyalty quotient. The significance of NPS is that it has a direct correlation on the future revenue growth of an entity.

So, *where is the difference between a brand ambassador and a brand advocate?*

The primary difference between a brand ambassador and brand advocacy is that a brand ambassador may not have an emotional connection for the brand but lends his/her image to a brand for a professional fee. On the other hand, brand advocacy has a strong emotional connection with the brand and strongly advocates people to buy a brand's products or services through word-of-mouth marketing.

Brand value is cumulative of the market cap, which is the tangible financial worth of a brand in the market, and the **brand equity,**

which is the intangible value added to the brand. Strong brand loyalty increases brand equity thereby increasing the brand value of an entity.

Quiz:

1. *Articulate the success of Mr. Barack Obama's US Presidential campaign in 2008 and Mr. Narendra Modi's campaign in 2014 with brand and branding terminologies.*
2. *A brand wants to increase brand loyalty quotient to thwart competition. What will be your advice?*
3. *Brand X recently launched a soap solution to remove all stains with just a few drops. The sales skyrocketed in the first few months and then dropped steeply. No new brands entered the market. The brand's product is available in stores without scarcity. Brand X appoints you as their new marketing manager. How will you proceed with the scenario?*
4. *A food brand has a legacy of 150 years delivering quality ready-to-eat food products in the market. It recently launched a new product in the market. Consumers suffered food poisoning due to the consumption of this new product. The brand's image was tarnished in the market and sales volume plummeted. It wants to stage a comeback in the market. The company appoints you as a consultant. How will you proceed with the scenario?*

Product Lifecycle

When an entity conceptualizes and manufactures a product, it travels through a product lifecycle, which is categorized into 4 stages. They are *market development stage, growth phase, maturity phase,* and *decline phase.*

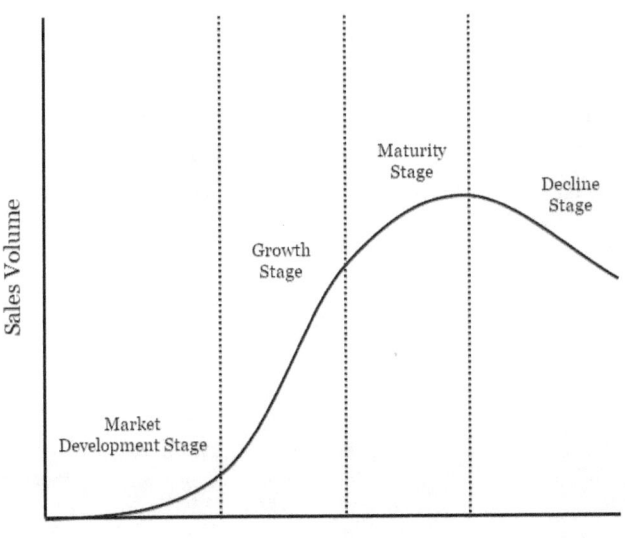

In the **market development stage,** the product is introduced into the market. Consumers are not aware of the product. There is hardly any demand for the product. An entity hardly makes any profit due to high initial investment, high promotional campaigns, and low sales turnover. Consumers who get attracted to the product in this stage are described as *innovators.*

In the **growth phase,** the product gains acceptance, the demand increases rapidly, the economies of scale improve, the distribution penetrates resulting in rapid sales turnover and profits. But competition increases, entities spend more on promotional campaigns to gain and retain market share. This reduces the profit margin. Consumers who get attracted in this stage are described as *early adopters.*

In the **maturity phase,** the product demand rate falls and the growth slows down. The competition gets intense. Entities reduce the price of the product to boost the demand. Some entities innovate or modify the product to boost sales. Consumers who get attracted in this stage are described as the *early majority.*

In the **decline phase,** there are hardly any consumers in the market. The demand rate falls drastically. Entities reduce promotional campaigns. The price of the product is reduced or more value is added to the product to tap sales. Some entities replace older products with newer products. Some entities plan to phase-out the product completely. Consumers who get attracted in this stage are described as the *late majority* and *laggards.*

Product Diffusion Curve

While the product lifecycle categorizes the product life journey in four stages, entities group consumers based on how quickly they accept products or services. This is because the consumers' risk preference is not the same. Some are risk-seekers, and some are risk-averse. The need/want for products or services also varies according to the socio-economic status of consumers. Hence, the adoption of products or services by consumers varies.

In his book "Diffusion of Innovations" written in 1962, Everett Rogers categorized consumers into five types as *innovators, early adopters, early majority, late majority,* and *laggards.*

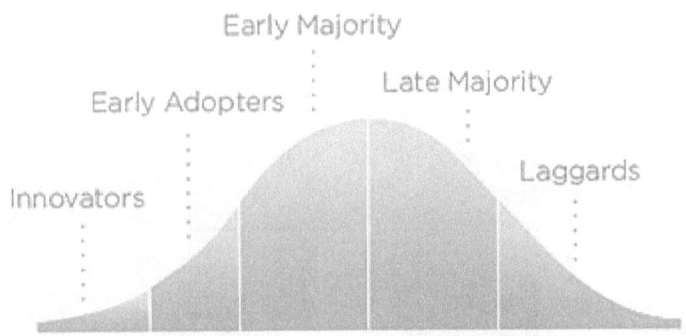

Innovators are influencers in the market with domain expertise and strong credibility with a fan following. They try out products or services free-of-cost or at cost price (without any profit). They do not add any value to the top-line of the business. They do reviews to influence their followers in buying products or services, but they may not be strong brand advocates to spread word-of-mouth in the market.

Early adopters are largely brand advocates who buy products or services to boost their egos and showcase their brand association. They are risk-seekers and spread word-of-mouth in the market for the brand. The buyers do not expect a higher value proposition. Entities use this brand loyalty and esteem/egoistic need to tap a premium price from early adopters.

Early Majority has an affinity for the brand but are not brand advocates. They like to hear about products or services from a trusted person, not from subject-matter experts or influencers, before buying. The buyers seek higher value propositions from products or services. Therefore, entities lower the premium prices to boost their value proposition.

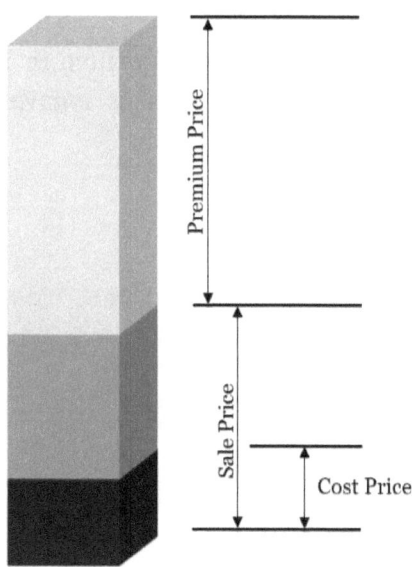

Late Majority are risk-averse, but not skeptical. They expect products or services to be visibly used in the market before they decide to buy. They are price-sensitive buyers looking for value-for-money and/or value-added-services.

Laggards are risk-averse and skeptical to let go of their products or services to adopt new products or services. They may have a brand association and brand loyalty to some other brands in the market, which makes it difficult for them to seek or accept products or services of another brand.

Quiz:

1. *Your start-up company is launching the first smartphone targeting the luxury segment. You conducted detailed primary market research. You are fairly confident that your luxury smartphone has a demand in the market and will meet the buyers' requirements. The problem is buyers do not know about your brand. You do not have any brand advocates. How will you create a brand to sell your luxury smartphone?*

Unique Selling Proposition, Value Proposition & Cost-Value Benefit

Imagine a brand selling deodorants or chocolates. The basic ingredients used by a brand and its competitors are almost the same. Then, why are they positioned differently and priced differently? And why do consumers develop a preference for a brand over competitors when the ingredients are almost the same?

The reasoning is because of the Unique Selling Proposition (USP) and Value Proposition expressed through cost-value-benefit.

The term – **Unique Selling Proposition (USP),** *also known as* **Unique Selling Points,** was first coined by Rosser Reeves, in 1961, in his book *"Reality in Advertising."*

USPs are a set of specific benefits that an entity claims that consumers get to experience by choosing its products or services over that of its competitors.

USPs of a brand are the features and technologies behind the products or services that are relatively non-copiable by competitors at least in the immediate future.

Most entities wrongly assume pricing, offers, discount, guarantees and warranties, return or replacement policy, and customer service as their USPs. They fail to understand that competitors can easily copy these offerings and decide to offer the same.

Sometimes brands do not have a distinct USP yet decide to formulate USPs for the sake of competition. It is perfectly fine if there are no USPs for the brand. They can still differentiate their products or services from that of competitors through brand legacy, brand attributes, brand promise, positioning, pricing, and value proposition.

The term **Value Proposition** was first coined by Michael Lanning and Edward Michaels in 1988 while consulting for McKinsey and Co.

Value Proposition changes for a buyer, for an employee, and for an investor.

> *When a brand compromises on the brand promise – what it stands for and what it promises to deliver, it compromises on its business!*

Value Proposition for a buyer is the value promised by an entity to its consumers when they use its products or services. The value promised is a mix of tangible performance and intangible experience. Value Proposition is a part of the brand promise.

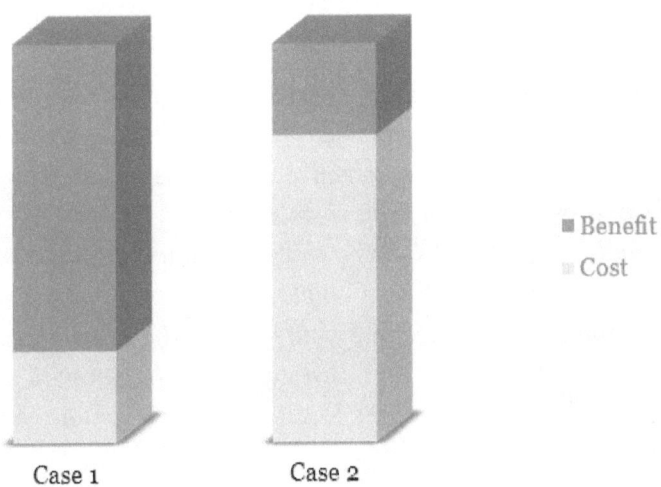

In the first case, a consumer experiences more benefits for the cost. The consumer feels more value received by using products or services and will be satisfied with the cost. The consumer develops a positive perception of the brand. In the second case, a consumer experiences lesser benefits and may not be satisfied with the cost. The consumer develops a negative perception of the brand.

Value Proposition for an employee is the value promised by an entity to its employees while in employment. The value is in terms of monetary and non-monetary benefits such as salary, perks, rewards, promotions, employee benefits, the brand they work for, and the satisfaction they derive in their work.

Value Proposition for an investor is the value promised by an entity to its investors for their investment. The value is in terms of measurable parameters such as market share, top-line revenue, bottom-line profits, earnings per stock, and non-measurable parameters such as brand creation as well as brand equity.

In simple words, the unique selling proposition is what makes an entity look differently better than that of its competitors. Whereas, the value proposition is why consumers have to buy a brand's products or services than that of competitors.

Quiz:

1. *You are owning a Brand X, which has an overwhelming market share of 65% in the previous year. Your buyers are strong brand advocates. The raw material cost increased by 20%. Fearing a drop in the demand, you decided not to pass on the burden to your loyal customers and switched to another supplier. You also reduced the perks of your employees to partly compensate for the raw material cost. Despite your action, the market share started dropping drastically. Your investor is not happy with the drop in the market share and asks to take corrective action. What will be your actions?*

Generic Products or Services

In the market research stage, an entity decides to produce either generic products/services or niche products/services depending on its business vision and mission. The demand for generic products or services is usually quite high and most of the time repetitive, and is, therefore, priced competitively by leveraging economies of scale in manufacturing. The segment is typically price sensitive. The drive for the sale is mostly impulsive shopping. Brand loyalty is relatively low though some may have varying levels of brand affinity. It is, therefore, essential for a brand to create top-of-the-mind brand awareness, brand recall, brand recognition as well as brand attributes to capture, retain, and increase the market share of the brand.

Quiz:

1. *Brand X is losing market share to a new entrant Brand Y. Brand X is the market leader and stopped advertising. Being the new entrant in the market, brand Y is vigorously advertising with amazing offers. Both brands are selling toothpaste to the same target consumer group. Brand X engages you to recapture the lost market. What will be your advice to Brand X?*

Niche Products or Services

Some entities conceptualize and design products or services to satisfy the esteem/egoistic needs of a very niche segment. The niche segment is generally small compared to the overall market size. The demand from the niche segment is also typically low and less repetitive. Poor economies of scale in manufacturing make products or services costlier and, therefore, charged at premium prices. The niche segment audience is less price sensitive. The drive for the sale is due to stronger brand attributes, brand association, brand affinity, brand loyalty, and brand value.

Quiz:

1. *A brand selling plain white rice launched organic rice. There are no direct competitors in the market for organic rice. You are hired to market organic rice in the market. Elucidate the steps for marketing organic rice.*

Cannibalization as a Marketing Strategy

Entities decide to launch a new line of offering along with the existing line of offering or decide to phase out the existing line of offerings. When an entity decides to phase out old products or services, it intentionally cannibalizes its existing line of products or services by introducing a new line of products or services. New products or services are designed to provide a better value proposition than the existing line of products or services so that people start preferring a new line of products or services. The market share for the new line of products or services increases to phase out the market share of the existing line of products or services.

Entities also stop innovating existing lines of products or services, and/or throttle supply of products or services, and/or halt manufacturing spare part components, and/or withdraw service repairs, thereby forcing people to upgrade to their new products or services. Consumers who are brand loyal upgrade without any hesitation. Consumers who have brand affinity but not brand loyalty upgrade with some level of reluctance. Consumers who are indifferent to brands start evaluating new products or services vis-à-vis that of competitors' offerings. Therefore, entities have to be careful about brand loyalty quotient while trying to cannibalize their products or services.

When an entity believes it has built a strong brand loyalty quotient, it might use **cannibalization of products or services** as a marketing strategy to gain market share by positioning its new line of products or services at an attractive price point yet provide or exceed the value proposition of competitors' products or services. This strategy to introduce a new line of products or services acts as a deterrent for competitors to build a brand loyalty quotient and even kill the competitors' market share.

But when an entity is selling products or services at a higher price point in the market, introducing new products or services at a lower price point in the same market can unintentionally and severely cannibalize its products or services that can lead to significant loss of market share and sales turnover for new and existing products or services. Brand loyal consumers may not like the brand to get diluted.

This can happen when consumers cannot experience the difference in the value proposition between products or services and choose a brand's new products or services for lower price points thereby displacing its existing products or services. The market share for new products or services might increase but the market share for existing products or services declines. Instead of increasing sales turnover, this unintentional erroneous move creates a severe loss to the business.

If an entity intentionally wants to introduce new products or services at a lower price point yet retain selling existing products or services, then it must clearly distinguish both the products or services through distinct brand identity, positioning, pricing, and value proposition to respective target consumer groups to avoid brand dilution and cannibalization.

In rare instances, when the market competition is intense or when the market is consolidated, an entity struggles to capture a bigger chunk of the market share. It deliberately uses **cannibalization of the market** as a marketing strategy to kill competitors' market share and even sacrifices its existing market share by introducing new products or services at a price point offering a higher value proposition to target consumers.

By this strategy, an entity can absorb its existing market share and the competitors' market share to become the new market leader. This is a dangerous ploy that might be extremely rewarding or a complete disaster for a brand.

Quiz:

1. *When the Indian mobile telecom sector was consolidating towards a few players, how was Reliance Jio able to capture a significant market share by beating the competition and even forcing dominant players to toe its line of business?*

2. *Did Xiaomi cannibalize the mobile phone market in India to become the market leader? After becoming the market leader, why did it introduce mobile phones under the brand POCO? Why was POCO made as a spin-off independent entity from Xiaomi?*

3. *An entity is a market leader in selling luxury watches. It wants to launch a new product line of affordable low-end watches in the same market. The entity is worried about the cannibalization of its luxury watch brand by introducing low-end watches. It is hiring you as an external marketing consultant to carry out this new product launch. How will you proceed?*

Fear of Missing Out as a Marketing Strategy

In the earlier topic, we learned that the degree of need/want and the hierarchy of the need/want as elucidated in **Maslow's hierarchy of needs** drive a sale.

Through the **product diffusion curve,** we understood that there are five categories of people – *innovators, early adopters, early majority, late majority,* and *laggards* and that late majority and laggards are risk-averse/skeptical about acceptance of new brand/product/technology.

If an entity is selling a high-involvement product, allowing the natural process of product diffusion takes time to reach the late majority and laggards. Entities have to wait longer to cover the market and/or recover their capital investment. So, how to quicken the buying decision among the late majority and laggards?

Marketers discovered in the behavioral psychology that consumers are largely insecure and anxious. The inability to get the want fulfilled makes them stressed out, at times leading to depression. With **fear-of-missing-out(FOMO) strategy,** entities tap this insecure feeling to create a perception in the minds of consumers that others are experiencing better life by using products or services and that he/she is missing out on experiencing that benefit.

Also, as learned in the product diffusion curve, consumers who fall under the late majority and laggards category procrastinate buying of products or services unless a sense of scarcity and urgency is created in their minds to buy soon. This FOMO strategy quickens up the absorption process for those who otherwise would wait longer.

A few techniques that can create FOMO are listed below:

- Launching soon
- Limited period offers
- Exclusive deals
- Offer till stocks last
- Offer valid for first few stock sales
- Free upgrade option for the first few stock sales
- Free delivery for first few stock sales
- Free delivery for a limited period
- Free add-on gift for first few stock sales
- Price increase after a few stock sales
- Limited period exchange offer
- Limited period cash back offers
- Display stocks sold
- Last chance to buy
- Highlight missed opportunities
- Highlight experiences of others

Market Dominance as a Marketing Strategy

There are four types of market dominance strategies – *market leader, market challenger, market follower,* and *market specialist.*

MARKET LEADER

In a mature market, where there are only a few competitors, an entity that has the largest market share in the market literally dominates competitors and even the consumers.

The market leader leads the pack in product innovation, product launch, product bundling, product pricing, product distribution, and product promotion. To ensure the market leader position, an entity might have to allocate a higher promotional budget than its competitors to fend-off any competition.

The competitors have fewer choices but to follow the path of the market leader to remain in the market. Consumers also have fewer choices but to accept predatory pricing as set by the market leader.

Sometimes, when the difference between the market leader and the market follower is ridiculously huge, the market leader position gives rise to **market monopoly.** In a market monopoly, one entity with its market leader position controls the market, knocks out the competition, and diminishes the choice for consumers. The monopoly entity sets the price and boosts its profits. To have a level-playing field, countries have enacted antitrust laws and consumer protection laws to curb anti-competitive practices.

Microsoft, Google, and many tech giants were penalized for leveraging their market monopoly to bundle software programs, which knocked out competitors giving fewer options for consumers.

MARKET CHALLENGER

In a market where there is no significant difference between market leader and market challenger, a market challenger can pose a serious threat to a market leader by innovating its product lines to launch new products and/or provide better value proposition than that of the market leader.

While the market leader spends more on promotions to maintain its market dominance, the market challenger provides similar products at a competitive price with a better value proposition to consumers.

When the market challenger believes that its new line of products is disruptive/innovative than the existing products in the market, the market challenger launches new products to attack the market leader's dominance to become the new market leader.

Sometimes, when a market leader tries to be assertive, the market challenger launches a counter-attack by increasing the value proposition of existing products in the market such as product bundling, free add-ons, that turns the table upside-down to become the new market leader.

MARKET FOLLOWERS

Unlike the market leader, market followers do not spend time, energy, and resources on product innovation as well as product promotion. Market followers follow the trend set by the market leader and the market challenger in launching their products to remain relevant in the market. They avoid a direct battle with the market leader.

On some rare occasions, the market follower launches an attack on the market leader through new product launches to become the new market leader.

MARKET SPECIALISTS

Market specialists are highly focused on a niche segment. They innovate products to cater to the demand of a niche segment. They do not compete or follow the market leader. They provide a different value proposition to their consumers. Often, these products have a premium price tag.

Quiz:

1. *Elucidate how Google ended the market dominance of Yahoo Mail and Hotmail in the web-based email service by introducing Gmail.*
2. *Elucidate how smartphones of Apple and Samsung killed the market dominance of Nokia and Blackberry.*

The Role of Advertisements & Advertising Platforms

> *Advertisements are an enabler to sell products or services and not a substitute for the products or services.*

Some entities presume that with deep-pockets for advertisements they can sell products or services to consumers without conducting market research and/or understanding the demand of the target consumer group. Some products have failed to gain sales volumes despite vigorous advertisement campaigns. Also, some products have succeeded in sales volumes without any paid advertisements. Entities fail to understand that advertisements are just an enabler to sell products or services. Advertisements reduce the dependency on the salesperson and the efficacy of the sales pitch, but it cannot be a substitute for the products or services. Therefore, an entity must focus on delivering the products or services that meet the demand of the consumers.

Despite having better products or services in the market, entities also fail to promote their products or services effectively. Entities must spend time in promotional activity as much as they spend on conceptualizing the products or services. Therefore, the main objectives of advertisements are to inform, persuade, create a positive perception, generate demand, and make prospective buyers brand loyal.

The promotional strategies vary according to the products or services. For brands that sell *low involvement products or services,* such as FMCG products, buyers do not spend much time on researching a brand as the products do not considerably affect their lifestyle and do not require significant investment to buy.

Brands leverage offline and online advertising platforms to mass communicate, create a brand, and spread awareness of products or services thereby generating demand. They generally do not carry a call-to-action sequence to the target consumer group.

For brands that sell *medium-to-high involvement products or services*, such as luxury cars, luxury watches, luxury jewels, or property, buyers spend time researching a brand to buy products that match their lifestyle as it requires a significant investment to buy.

Brands leverage offline and online advertising platforms to mass communicate and/or personally persuade consumers on brand legacy, brand promise, brand attributes, brand value, unique selling proposition, value proposition, pricing and offers to buy their products or services. They generally carry a clear call-to-action sequence to the target consumer group such as a *call for a demo, call to know more, visit a showroom, visit a website,* or *download an app* and make them buy a brand's products or services.

Types of Advertisements

Proctor & Gamble was the first to classify advertisements as above-the-line (ATL) advertisements and below-the-line (BTL) advertisements in 1954.

Above-the-line (ATL) advertisements are for brand building exercise – for creating brand awareness, for increasing brand recall/brand recognition/brand visibility as well as for increasing and/or restoring brand reputation (image and goodwill) among the masses.

This kind of advertisement has a wider reach but to a largely untargeted audience with a high spillover rate. Lead generation is not the prime objective of ATL advertisements. Therefore, ATL advertisements do not carry a call-to-action sequence.

Typical ATL advertising platforms are television, radio, newspaper as well as out-of-home (OOH) advertising options such as billboards, lamp poles, center medians, and on the outside bodies of public transport vehicles.

The effectiveness of ATL advertisements is gauged by an increase in brand awareness, brand recall, brand recognition, brand visibility, and brand reputation.

Below-the-line (BTL) advertisements involve direct interaction with prospective buyers. BTL advertisements are used when the target consumer group is identified and is concentrated in the desired location. The spillover rate and the cost of advertisement are lower in BTL advertisements compared to ATL advertisements.

Lead generation and persuasion of prospective buyers are prime objectives of BTL advertisements. Therefore, BTL advertisements have a specific call-to-action sequence.

Typical offline BTL advertising involves employing a trained salesperson or an agency to carry door-to-door pamphlet distribution, sales demonstration, telemarketing, conduct roadshows and tradeshows, point-of-sale (POS) promotions, direct mailing, or messaging.

Typical online BTL advertising involves email marketing, social media advertising, and search engines advertising with audience targeting to drive traffic to a website or an app to generate leads and to increase storefront visits.

The effectiveness of BTL advertisements is gauged by sales volume, conversion rates, footfalls to storefront/roadshows/tradeshows, open rates of emails and messages, increase in website traffic, or the number of app downloads.

The merits of ATL advertisements and BTL advertisements are combined in **Through-the-line (TTL) advertisements.**

Unlike an ATL advertisement, a TTL advertisement aims at a wider reach of a targeted audience and is conversion-focused by including a specific call-to-action sequence in the advertisement.

High-involvement products or services, luxury goods, and niche products or services generally use TTL advertisements.

The effectiveness of TTL advertisements is gauged by an increase in brand awareness, brand recall, brand recognition, brand visibility, brand reputation, lead generation, sale conversion, sale volume, and return-on-marketing investment.

Quiz:

1. *Brand X has a 70% market share in the noodles segment. It recently encountered a food safety problem, which created negative publicity in the market. The market share plummeted to less than*

10%. Brand X is consulting you to recapture the market share. What will your plan of action be?

2. *Brand Y is planning to launch a new variety of dairy products in the market where they are supplying milk. You are the marketing head. You have been asked to design a marketing campaign with a constrained marketing budget. Specify your course of action.*

Types of Advertising Platforms

Traditional forms of advertising platforms included painting on walls, newspapers, billboards, and pamphlets distribution.

With the invention of the radio and television, advertising platforms shifted gears by taking advertisements right into homes of consumers.

Entities then employed salespeople to be in direct touch with consumers through telemarketing, door-to-door marketing, direct mailing, tradeshows, or roadshows to sell their products or services.

With the dawn of the internet era and disruptive technologies, entities started selling their products or services through a website, email, search engine platforms, and social media platforms.

This evolution of advertising platforms and the power of the internet made people believe that marketing has changed over a period. In reality, advertising platforms are evolving with time. Marketers are leveraging new and evolving platforms to advertise their products or services.

Just for the sake of simplicity, marketers group the technological shift in advertising platforms under traditional marketing, digital marketing, and futuristic marketing.

Traditional marketing is offline advertising (without using the internet) through the above-the-line (ATL), below-the-line (BTL), and through-the-line (TTL) platforms in *newspapers, billboards, pamphlets distribution, direct mailing, telemarketing, door-to-door marketing, tradeshows,* or *roadshows.*

Digital marketing is advertising using electronic equipment with or without the power of the internet. People often get confused between digital marketing and online marketing. **Online marketing** is a *subset* of digital marketing where it uses electronic gadgets and the power of the internet to advertise.

Some examples of offline digital advertising (advertising through electronic equipment without internet) are advertising on television, radio, and *electronic OOH (out-of-home) platforms.*

Some examples of online digital advertising (advertising through electronic gadgets with the internet) are email marketing, website, social media advertising, search engine advertising, podcasts, and *eBooks.*

Futuristic marketing is advanced digital marketing using Big Data Analytics and Predictive Marketing – making machines dissect and interpret the data through Machine Learning (ML) and performing actions through Artificial Intelligence (AI).

Some of the examples are chatbots, facial recognition, image search, online virtual assistant, voice-assisted virtual assistant, dynamic pricing, automated ad targeting, and *automated content curation.*

Quiz:

1. *Digital wallets and online payments have gathered steam recently. Tech giants Google Inc, Apple Inc, Amazon Inc and Facebook Inc are actively pursuing non-core business verticals such as digital wallets, selling smartwatches, smart shoes, fitness gadgets, and smart speakers? What is the necessity to launch these products? How will these products help entities in their core business?*

2. *What is the necessity for Apple Inc and Amazon Inc to launch their standalone credit cards when they are already in the digital wallet space? How will these products help entities in their core business?*

Outbound Marketing and Inbound Marketing

Outbound marketing is a traditional method of pushing products or services into the market through ads in search of prospective buyers.

Entities use print and broadcast media platforms, OOH platforms, social media platforms, search engine display platforms, content discovery platforms, carry out telemarketing and door-to-door sales, participate in tradeshows, roadshows, send emails, and message blasts to a sourced database.

The author likes to educate book readers that sourcing a database without the consent of the person involved for any purpose let alone for advertising is against one's privacy. It is an unethical intrusion that can have serious legal implications for the brand. Therefore, the author cautions against sourcing such databases for advertising.

Outbound marketing is a non-interactive one-way communication where non-prospective buyers might feel the ads are irrelevant, interruptive, and annoying. Therefore, outbound marketing is less productive and expensive.

Content is the King.

The internet has revolutionized the way buyers shop for products or services. Buyers of this era want to have complete control of the information that they search for or seek. Buyers search for reviews by subject-matter experts, opinions of social media influencers, and even do self-research before they buy a product. This shift in shopping behavior led the way for inbound marketing.

Inbound marketing is a relatively new phenomenon where entities pull prospective buyers through enriched content, provide an option to opt-in for newsletters/white papers/emails/webinars/podcasts/blogs/vlogs/infographics/eBooks, subscribe to social media pages and channels, and later focus on converting the traffic into leads and leads into sales through the power of content marketing.

Inbound marketing is an interactive two-way communication where prospective buyers feel the content is relevant, interesting, engaging, informative, and adding value. Inbound marketing creates a positive perception of the brand. Prospective buyers may not feel the content annoying as they have opted for it and they find it useful. Therefore, inbound marketing is more productive and cost-effective in the long run but takes time to build subscribers or followers.

To make it simple, in outbound marketing, marketers desperately seek the attention of prospective buyers to make a sale. In inbound marketing, marketers earn the respect of prospective buyers through powerful content and then convert.

Quiz:

1. Why *do pharmacy apps have content on doctors' advice, herbal products, health hygiene, health nutrition, or stretch-out exercises? Also, why do they provide an option to consult a doctor online, book an appointment online, and even book a cab for the appointment?*

The Dawn of Online Marketing and Beyond

The power of the internet has connected people across the length and breadth of the world. With the discovery of electronic gadgets such as *smartphones* and *tablets,* businesses can connect with consumers or other businesses to advertise and be in constant communication with their clients (consumers as well as other businesses) of their products or services.

As one keeps visiting websites and apps, entities ask visitors to give consent to collect, use, and even share digital footprints such as *demographics, geography, interests, behaviors, affinity, values,* and *beliefs* for their use and use by third parties. These digital footprints are used by the entities to target consumers in social media platforms and search engine platforms.

Social media platforms are primarily demand generation platforms where people are shown ads by interrupting while they are hanging out on these platforms. *Some of the social media platforms are Facebook, Instagram, LinkedIn, Twitter,* and *Tik Tok.* Each platform targets a set of audiences offering a different set of experiences. It is, therefore, necessary for marketers to understand the psychology of the audience for each social media platform and leverage the same to the best advantage.

Search engine platforms are primarily demand fulfillment platforms where people actively look for products or services on the web. *Some of the search engine platforms are Google, YouTube, Bing,* and *Yahoo.*

An entity can reach out to consumers who are looking for products or services with the help of browsing history, search history, IP, tracking codes, and cookies.

Both these platforms provide campaigns for creating awareness, for increasing traffic to website/app, for lead generation, and for sales conversion.

In recent years, **content discovery platforms** have gained traction as they curate personalized content for consumers based on consumers' metadata. These platforms also allow consumers to explore new topics without having to search on the internet by seamlessly integrating into a website. *Some of the content discovery platforms are Taboola, Outbrain,* and *Colombia.*

Consumers' data is a treasure trove for businesses!

Social media platforms, search engine platforms, and content discovery platforms have a wealth of information about you than you would ever imagine. In everyday life, you are giving away so much information about your geography, demography, interest, behaviors, affinity, belief, values. More and more data points about consumers are made available for brands to target. Machines are made smarter to dissect, learn, interpret, and predict the behavioral pattern of consumers. The degree of each of your attributes about interest, behaviors, affinity, belief, and values are improvised continuously through machine learning.

Big Data Analytics, Machine Learning, and *Artificial Intelligence* have already changed the way brands communicate with their consumers. Consumers have also embraced the concept of utilizing an *online virtual assistant,* which can track, monitor, and assist people in their daily tasks.

So next time when you like or react to a social media post, **and/or** when you follow a group or a page in social media, **and/or** when you visit a website or a blog, **and/or** when you add a life event such as birthdays/anniversaries/single/engaged/married/divorced/complicated/became a parent, **and/or** when you tag a place you tour or check-in, **and/or** when you watch a video from Netflix and its competitors, **and/or** when you hear a song from Spotify and its competitors, **and/or** when you create an account using Facebook or Google or any other brands, **and/or** when you make a transaction through a digital wallet, remember you are giving away data points that can be tracked, processed, and leveraged by marketers.

With so much data available in the public domain and the explicit access that you provide while signing up for an account, machines collate data points to understand your needs, map your brain functioning, and targets ads with personalized communication. As people are irrational in their behavior, one can be triggered or made to feel insecure to make them buy products or services.

Artificial Intelligence predicts solutions for consumers' problems even before consumers are aware of it.

- *Imagine if a smartwatch tracks the heartbeat/sleep pattern of a user daily and alerts a user for a health check-up when it observed an irregular or changed heartbeat/sleep pattern for some time.*
- *Imagine if a smartwatch user suddenly fell unconscious with no movements for some time, the smartwatch detects and sends an SOS as well as GPS location to the user's emergency contacts seeking help.*
- *Imagine you are chatting with your friend asking opinion about a product and the product review by influencers or subject matter experts crops up on your browser screen automatically.*
- *Imagine your mom is complaining to you to repair the air conditioner. Your voice-assistant listens and shows up an air-conditioner repair ad on your mobile from your locality.*
- *Imagine you are out of your home and an electrical fire starts in your home. The online virtual assistant detects the abnormal and sudden temperature rise in the rooms and alerts you as well as the local fire department with GPS location.*

However, of late, there has been rampant misuse and/or intrusion of data and consent given to these technologies as well as misuse by hackers, which has forced governments across the world to take preventive and protective measures against the breach/violation of data privacy and data security. Many tech giants have also been penalized for intentional and unintentional breach/violation of data privacy and data security. This makes some users cautious about giving real information.

Why email marketing will stay forever!

Social media platforms, search engine platforms, content discovery platforms, and futuristic technologies will keep evolving. Some platforms will gain popularity, reach their peak, and then lose traction. Some platforms may fade away with time, thus time, money, and effort that brands invested to build traction become pointless. Brands do not have control over third-party platforms. The only platforms that brands own and control are their website/app and the database generated through the website/app/offline inquiry forms. Therefore, brands must include email marketing and telemarketing despite new technological advances/newer platforms.

Quiz:

1. *Name the Acts legislated by various governments in the world to safeguard their citizens against breach/violation of data privacy and data security.*

Types of Audience Targeting in Online Marketing

Online advertisement platforms provide various targeting options for entities to target consumers based on *demographics, geography, keyword, search history, behavior, interest, context, placement, time-period,* and *technology* that are available in the public domain and consented for.

In **demographics targeting,** entities target to sell their products or services to consumers based on *their age, gender, race, religion, ethnicity, language, marital status, parental status, education, occupation, income levels, company worked for,* and *company working for.*

In **geo-targeting,** entities target to sell their products or services to consumers based on *the country, city, pin code,* or *radius* where consumers currently reside in and/or where consumers show an interest in. Entities also target consumers based on *recently traveled from, recently traveled to,* and *expats of a country* to sell their products or services.

In **keyword targeting,** entities target to sell products or services when consumers search for products or services in search engines.

In **search history** targeting, entities target to sell their products or services to consumers based on the keyword searches or website visits in the past. Entities also target to sell their products or services to consumers who visited their competitors' websites/apps/social media accounts in the past.

In **behavioral targeting,** entities target to sell their products or services to consumers based on the type of *websites/apps they visit for shopping, the session time spent, the page-depth scrolled, engagement levels,* and *buying patterns.* The best examples of behavioral targeting are *recommended products or services in eCommerce websites, recommended pages in social media platforms, recommended posts in blogs or news portals.*

In **interest targeting,** entities target to sell their products or services to consumers based on *their lifestyle, food, sports, fitness, beauty, wellness, entertainment, hobbies, business, industry, profession, politics,* or *religion.*

In **contextual (topic) targeting,** entities target to sell products or services closely associated to a page or blog that consumers visit with an assumption that consumers might be interested to buy their products or services – *displaying ads of women beauty products to people when they visit women wellness blogs or websites, displaying ads of sports gear to people when they visit sports blogs or websites,* or *displaying health check-up ads to people when they visit fitness blogs or websites.*

In **placement targeting,** entities target to sell their products or services when consumers visit specific websites/apps.

In **time-period targeting,** entities target to sell their products or services during a particular day and/or hour in a week.

In **technology targeting,** entities target consumers based on *the device type (desktops, mobiles,* or *tablets), operating system type, operating system version, browser type, browser version, mobile network carriers,* or *screen resolution* to sell their products or services.

Quiz:

1. *A relatively unknown online ticket selling brand wants to increase the sale of tickets for movies, concerts, and events in the city. You have been tasked to design a promotional campaign to achieve the business goals. How will you proceed?*

Learning Sales Funnel

When a brand advertises its products or services, some prospective buyers have an intrinsic demand and inquire. Some look at an advertisement, feel the products or services may be useful, and inquire to know more. Some look at an advertisement and immediately skip it as they do not have any need/want for such products or services. The degree of demand for products or services varies among the target consumer group.

Therefore, a prospect goes through 3 stages – *Awareness Stage, Consideration Stage,* and *Conversion Stage* – for buying products or services. Here, a prospect is classified based on awareness, interest, and intent levels. This is called **Sales Funnel,** *also known as* **Buying Cycle.**

Not every prospect is ready to buy products or services immediately.

In the **Awareness Stage,** a target consumer group is made aware of the brand's products or services, how it can solve consumers' problem, and make them feel the need/want through ATL and TTL advertisements by highlighting on the brand, positioning, unique selling proposition, value proposition.

Prospects are rated based on their interest, desire, and intent levels when they inquire about the brand's products or services. A simplistic approach most entities follow is to rate prospects based on *Hot, Warm, Cold,* and *Dead.* This step is called **Lead Scoring.**

- Hot – a desire with a strong and immediate intent to buy
- Warm – a desire without a strong/immediate intent to buy
- Cold – just an inquiry with some amount of interest
- Dead – just an inquiry with no interest

As prospects are scored by the salespeople, there can be differences in the lead scoring pattern for a similar prospect. To eliminate human flaw in the lead scoring, entities innovate lead scoring techniques as per their convenience and train their salesperson so that they rate uniformly.

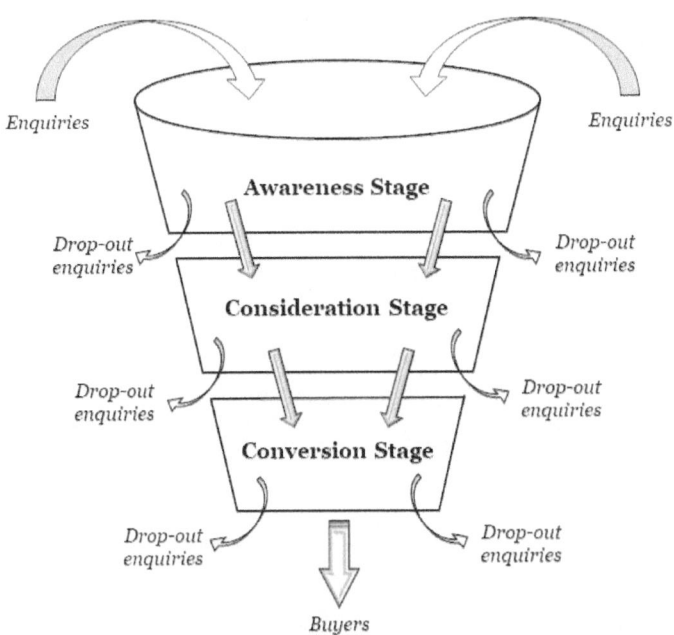

In the **Consideration Stage,** a consumer is nurtured carefully *through an email or SMS sequence, through telecalls by salespeople, through automatic ad sequence in online platforms, by giving free trial samples,* or *by giving a demo of products or services* to quicken the decision-making. Customer reviews, social reputation, and testimonials also facilitate decision-making. This step is called **Lead Nurturing.**

In the **Conversion Stage,** entities rollout discount offers, cash back offers, money-back guarantees, or replacement guarantees as a last-minute push to the target consumer group to close the sale.

Products or services that fall under safety needs, egoistic or esteem needs, and high-involvement products or services require an aggressive **Sales Pitch** in the Consideration Stage and the Conversion Stage for sales conversion.

Quiz:

1. *You are an owner of a Brand X, which earlier introduced a product A in the market with much fanfare. The product demand fizzled out in just a few months. You are re-launching the same product with some modifications in the same market. People are apprehensive to buy your product. What will be your plan of action?*

Ingredients of an Effective Sales Pitch

Products or services that fall under physiological needs may not require any effort to sell. Whereas for products or services that fall under safety needs, egoistic or esteem needs, and high-involvement products or services, a salesperson must induce serious "desire and intent" in the minds of prospective buyers before selling products or services. This step of inducing "desire and intent" by the salesperson in the minds of consumers is known as **Sales Pitch,** *also known as* **Elevator Pitch.**

When a prospective buyer visits a storefront, or when a salesperson telecalls or visits a prospective buyer's home or meets in tradeshows or roadshows, the primary objective of a salesperson is to understand what the demand is, whether the demand is intrinsic, and the degree of the demand.

Once a salesperson understands the demand of prospective buyers, one must start pitching for products or services revolving around the brand, the brand's positioning, the unique selling proposition, the value proposition, and making a convincing case for prospective buyers to buy the products or services. A sales pitch has to be short, precise, and concise in its delivery.

An effective sales pitch must have the following ingredients:

1. Tell a story of the brand legacy – of satisfying buyers' demand with products or services to engage with the prospective buyers.
2. Elucidate the problems faced by the buyers, explain how new products or services can ease the buyers' life and/or how it can resolve buyers' grievances/meet buyers' expectations.
3. Showcase independent researches, subject matter expert reviews, and customer reviews to convey the point.
4. Tell how new products or services are better than or different from the existing line of products or services.
5. Tell how new products or services are better than or different from the competitors' products or services – in terms of positioning, unique selling proposition, value proposition, pricing, customer service, and other clear differentiators.
6. Focus on the brand promise and roll-out enticing offers such as free demos, free trial samples, discount offers, cash back offers, free shipping, money-back guarantees, or replacement guarantees.
7. End the sales pitch open-ended to allow prospective buyers to pose questions.

Generally, entities engage specialized agencies for conducting market research and for marketing communications. It is seen in some cases the reason why entities conceptualized products or services based on their market research are not wholly captured in the marketing communications and/or in the sales pitch. If the brand's positioning, unique selling proposition, value proposition, how their products or services can fulfill the demand of the buyers are not articulated credibly, then prospective buyers may not get fully convinced to buy. Therefore, entities must be careful in their marketing communications and sales pitch.

Also, if a salesperson is not trained in the sales pitch, he/she will remain defensive even as a prospective buyer leads the discussion. In such a scenario, the salesperson ends up merely answering queries of the prospective buyer. The salesperson would miss the opportunity to put across a convincing sales pitch of how the brand's products or services are better and why the prospective buyer must buy it. Therefore, training a salesperson in the sales pitch is an essential activity, which most entities least focus on.

The only way to deliver a power-packed sales pitch is perfecting this art through several practices. A salesperson must be trained to understand the demand of the prospective buyer and then lead the discussion by developing an instant rapport with the prospective buyer so that the prospective buyer listens about the brand, its new products or services, its competitors and their offerings in order to make a convincing case of how its products or services are better and why a prospective buyer must buy it.

The salesperson must also gauge the pulse of the prospective buyer and categorize the prospective buyer as *hot, warm, cold,* and *dead.* This will help the sales team to focus on prospective buyers, who show more intent to buy. Meanwhile, entities can focus on prospective buyers, who are categorized as warm or cold through remarketing and retargeting techniques to move them down in the sales funnel.

Importance of Remarketing and Retargeting

In every stage of the sales funnel, some inquiries drop-out for various reasons. Entities must re-engage with drop-out prospects with remarketing and retargeting techniques to identify if the desire and intent levels of some prospects can be increased and pursued for sales closure.

Before the start of the explosive social media era, there was only remarketing. Prospects provided a postal address, email and contact numbers during a visit to a storefront or in a tradeshow or a roadshow. During the launch of new products or services and/or to follow-up with prospects, who previously inquired, entities sent personalized emails/calls or postal mails to re-engage with *existing active* and/or *inactive* prospects. This engagement is termed as **Remarketing.**

In **Retargeting,** entities target prospects who visited a website or a mobile app and took some actions such as visiting a page, adding to cart, or downloading eBrochure/eBook through social media platforms and/or search engine platforms and re-engage with them.

A website or a mobile app is designed with tracking codes provided by social media platforms and search engine platforms. When a prospect visits a website or a mobile app, a cookie gets installed on the prospect's electronic device through the user's explicit consent. Digital footprints help entities to target and re-engage with prospective buyers to complete the sales funnel. Retargeting is to identify *new* prospects.

With the dawn of the internet era, entities have started collecting prospects' details during signup or login registration process when they visit a website or a mobile app. This detail is used for remarketing.

Is remarketing and retargeting the same? What is the difference?

Many marketers believe remarketing and retargeting to be the same – to re-engage with prospects for the completion of sales funnel, but there is a slight difference between the two.

In remarketing, an entity possesses details of prospects such as postal addresses, email contacts, and contact numbers whereas in retargeting, an entity does not possess details of visitors but targets using digital footprints. For this, tracking codes and cookies are to be installed on visitors' electronic devices for retargeting, whereas tracking codes and cookies are not required for remarketing.

The difference between retargeting and remarketing gets diluted when social media platforms and search engine platforms allow entities to upload the subscribed database of emails and mobile numbers so that entities can retarget the prospects through their platforms.

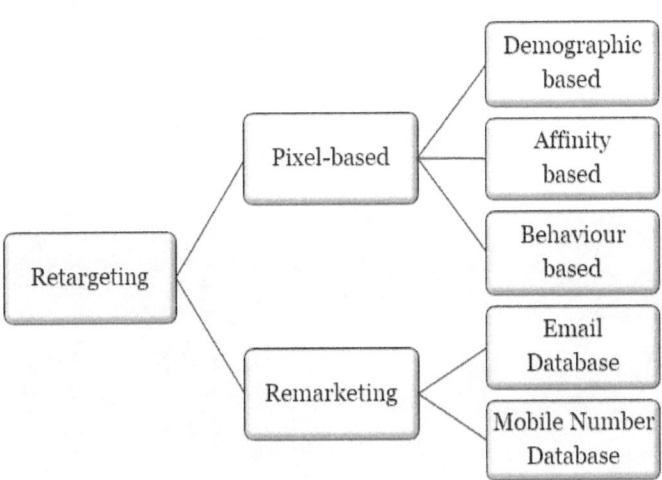

Using tracking codes and cookies, entities target prospects based on their geography, demography, interest, affinity, behavior, values, device types, search history, and even database-matching. Tracking codes and cookies also help entities to target prospects in cross platforms *(for example, targeting prospects who visited a website and retargeting the prospect on a Social Media Platform)*, cross devices *(for example, targeting prospects who visited from a laptop and retargeting the prospect on a mobile)* and even competitors' online platforms *(for example, retargeting prospects who visited competitors' website or app in social media and search engine platforms)*.

Entities leverage remarketing and retargeting techniques to greatly reduce the cost of marketing and in-turn increase the return-on-marketing investment.

Financial Metrics in Marketing

Marketers must periodically evaluate the effectiveness of the marketing campaign using a few metrics and take suitable corrective action if necessary. There are several financial metrics in marketing. However, the following metrics are frequently used by marketers.

Cost per thousand impressions (CPM) is a metric to determine the marketing cost incurred to generate a thousand ad impressions. This metric was in existence even before the advent of online marketing to measure CPM for ads in television/radio/email marketing campaigns.

$$CPM = \frac{Marketing\ spend}{Number\ of\ ad\ impressions\ ('000)}$$

Cost per inquiry (CPI) is a metric to determine the marketing cost incurred to generate an inquiry. Not every inquiry can be considered as a lead. The inquirers might be prospective buyers for some other products or services, or the inquiry might be casual or junk or has a different requirement. Say, when you advertise a product or service, entities receive inquiries seeking jobs, vendors, distributors, retailers, and even competitors.

$$CPI = \frac{Marketing\ spend}{Number\ of\ inquiries\ generated}$$

Cost per lead (CPL) is a metric to determine the marketing cost incurred to generate a unique prospective lead.

$$CPL = \frac{Marketing\ spend}{Number\ of\ unique\ prospective\ leads\ generated}$$

Cost per sale conversion (CPS) is a metric to determine the marketing cost incurred to generate a sale.

$$CPS = \frac{Marketing\ spend}{Number\ of\ sale\ closures}$$

Return-on-marketing investment (ROMI) is a metric to measure the incremental revenue generated because of the incremental marketing spend divided by the incremental marketing spend. ROMI is different from return-on-investment (ROI), which includes capital investment in the form of plant and machinery.

$$ROMI = \frac{Incremental\ revenue\ growth - Incremental\ marketing\ spend}{Incremental\ marketing\ spend}$$

Customer lifetime value (CLV) is a metric to determine the lifetime worth (spend) of a consumer for a brand.

$$CLV = Average\ value\ of\ a\ sale$$
$$* Number\ of\ times\ a\ consumer\ buys\ in\ a\ year$$
$$* Average\ retention\ time\ for\ a\ typical\ consumer$$

Quiz:

1. *Assume you ran a promotional campaign for the launch of a new product. Calculate CPM, CPI, CPL, CPS, ROMI for the following:*

	Television	Newspaper	Social Media
Spend	$40,000	$40,000	$20,000
Ad Impressions	300,000	100,000	450,000
Inquiries	20	40	120
Prospective Leads	2	4	70
Sale Conversion	0	1	7

2. *Your firm is selling toddler and children's toys up to the age of 10. The average value of a toddler toy per sale is $40 and the average value of a children's toy per sale is $20. A customer buys toddler toys four times in a year and children's toys twice in a year. Estimate customer lifetime value.*

Understanding the Economics for Marketing

Economics greatly influence the marketing of products or services. Therefore, marketers must understand economics to devise their marketing strategies and to allocate resources accordingly.

Economies of scale, supply-demand imbalance, demand fluctuations, and stock-keeping can influence the marketing strategies of products or services.

ADVANTAGE OF ECONOMIES OF SCALE

Consumers wonder why niche products or luxury products cost more and why generic products cost less. This is primarily due to economies of scale in production. Economies of scale give a competitive advantage for entities that have larger production capacities over that of smaller production capacities.

Entities that produce generic products generally have larger production capacities. The larger production capacities allow entities to produce goods in large quantities. As entities manufacture more goods, the fixed capital investment recovery is spread over more goods produced. Also, the production process becomes more efficient at some scale of operations due to cost-saving from bulk imports of raw materials; and/or better utilization of manpower; and/or optimum utilization as well as manufacturing efficiencies of equipment in the production lines; and/or cost-saving from bulk transportation; and/or cost-saving from bulk media space buying. These factors help in lowering the cost per unit produced as the production increases. Entities can leverage this economy of scale to lower the sale value of goods.

Entities that produce niche products or luxury products may not have economies of scale due to lower production capacities. To recover the fixed capital investment, entities distribute the fixed capital investment over a small number of goods produced and this makes the cost of production higher. Entities may also find it difficult to save costs on raw materials import, manpower utilization, warehousing, transportation, and media space buying.

To leverage economies of scale in production, entities that produce niche products or luxury products outsource some of the production of goods to ancillary entities, who can manufacture part components at better manufacturing efficiencies.

For example, automobile manufacturing companies outsource the manufacturing of gears, batteries, engines, tires, and seats to auto ancillary companies, who can leverage economies of scale. Auto companies can restrict their business to manufacturing car/bus chassis and integrating ancillary components to deliver quality goods. This outsourcing strategy reduces the overall cost of goods produced.

Quiz:

1. *An entity enters a new market where consumers are not aware of the brand to launch its first product in the market. It sets up a manufacturing unit at a cost of $1 billion with a production capacity of 1 million units per year. The entity intends to recover the installation cost and make a cumulative profit of $300 million in 7 years. The market research team suggests that the average sale price of the competitor is $1,500 per unit. It also suggests that the sale price cannot increase by more than 1% every year. Assume marketing cost, admin cost, overhead cost, storage cost, and freight*

cost add to $50 per unit produced in the first year and increases 10% every year. The economies of scale data are presented below:

Units, in millions	Average Cost per Unit
0.10	$2,800
0.20	$2,000
0.30	$1,400
0.40	$1,000
0.50	$800
0.60	$700
0.70	$670
0.80	$650
0.90	$650
1.00	$680

The demand forecast for first 7 years are 0.20, 0.35, 0.55, 0.75, 0.75, 0.80, 0.80 million units, respectively. Fix a sale price for the product to calculate sales turnover and profits year-on-year.

IMPORTANCE OF DEMAND FORECASTING

Demand forecasting is a scientific method of estimating future demand for products or services based on the historical sales volume, the selling price of products or services, the purchasing power of consumers, changes in the industry competition, and the future economic outlook.

Demand forecasting helps entities to plan for production volumes, to devise advertising strategies, pricing strategies, to optimize stock-keeping in the distribution channel and even to plan for recruitment or retrenchment of permanent/temporary staff.

Demand forecasting is carried as a *short-run demand forecast* (typically for 1–12 months) and *long-run demand forecast* (typically for 1–10 years).

Demand forecasting must account for seasonal variations in the demand caused due to climate, weather, festivities, holidays. Cyclical demand variation is due to economic conditions that usually lasts for more than a year where a business undergoes rise, peak, decline, and recession at regular intervals.

Demand forecasting is unpredictable and irregular during and aftermath of disastrous events such as earthquakes, tsunami, epidemic, floods, drought, or war.

UNDERSTANDING ELASTICITY IN DEMAND

Elasticity in demand is when the demand for the products changes either due to the change in the price of products or due to change in income levels of consumers.

In the **price-inelastic demand,** the demand for the product changes little when the price of the product increases or decreases. Products that fall under physiological need and safety need are mostly inelastic as they form the basic need for human survival and well-being.

Examples: Food items, medicines, fuel, cigarettes, salt, sugar, or chocolates are neither affected due to change in the price of products nor due to change in income levels of consumers.

In **price-elastic demand,** the demand for the product changes drastically when the price of the product changes.

Examples: The sale of bikes, cars, television sets, mobile handsets, or furniture, which are affected by a change in the price of the products even when the income levels of consumers have not changed much.

In **cross-price elastic demand,** the demand for the product changes with a change in the price of another product assuming that income levels of consumers have not changed much. The product might act as complementary or as a substitute for the product considered.

Examples of complementary goods – An increase in the sale of mobile handsets increases the demand for SIM card connection. Similarly, an increase in the sale of photocopier printing machines increases the demand for ink cartridges. When the price of mobile handsets and printers are reduced, people buy more, and this demand leads to increased demand for new SIM card connections or ink cartridges, respectively.

Examples of substitute goods – It is generally considered vegetables are a substitute for meat. When the price of meat increases, people start consuming more vegetables. The demand for vegetables increases with an increase in the price of meat. Similarly, when the subscription price of Microsoft 365 increases, people look for alternative office suites such as Google Docs or Zoho Office Suite.

In **income-elastic demand,** real incomes of consumers affect the demand for products even when the prices of the products have not changed.

Examples are high-involvement products such as purchasing a property, car, gold, or luxury watches, where consumers change their buying decision when their income levels change drastically.

INVENTORY MANAGEMENT

A manufacturer produces goods and supplies to wholesalers, who in turn supply to retailers for end-consumers to buy. Therefore, a distribution network is an interconnected group of players involving manufacturers, wholesalers, and retailers in the movement of produced goods to end consumers. The supply chain also focuses on raw material supply network so that a manufacturer does not suffer from want of raw materials when demand is peaking.

An entity must optimize its distribution network, based on demand forecasting, so that the demand for goods is fulfilled to end consumers without any scarcity or surplus.

This is achieved by adjusting its production by accounting for stocks in the warehouse, stocks with wholesalers, stocks with retailers, and the goods-in-transit through stock-keeping units (SKU), *which is a scannable alphanumeric bar code to track the movement of goods in the distribution network.*

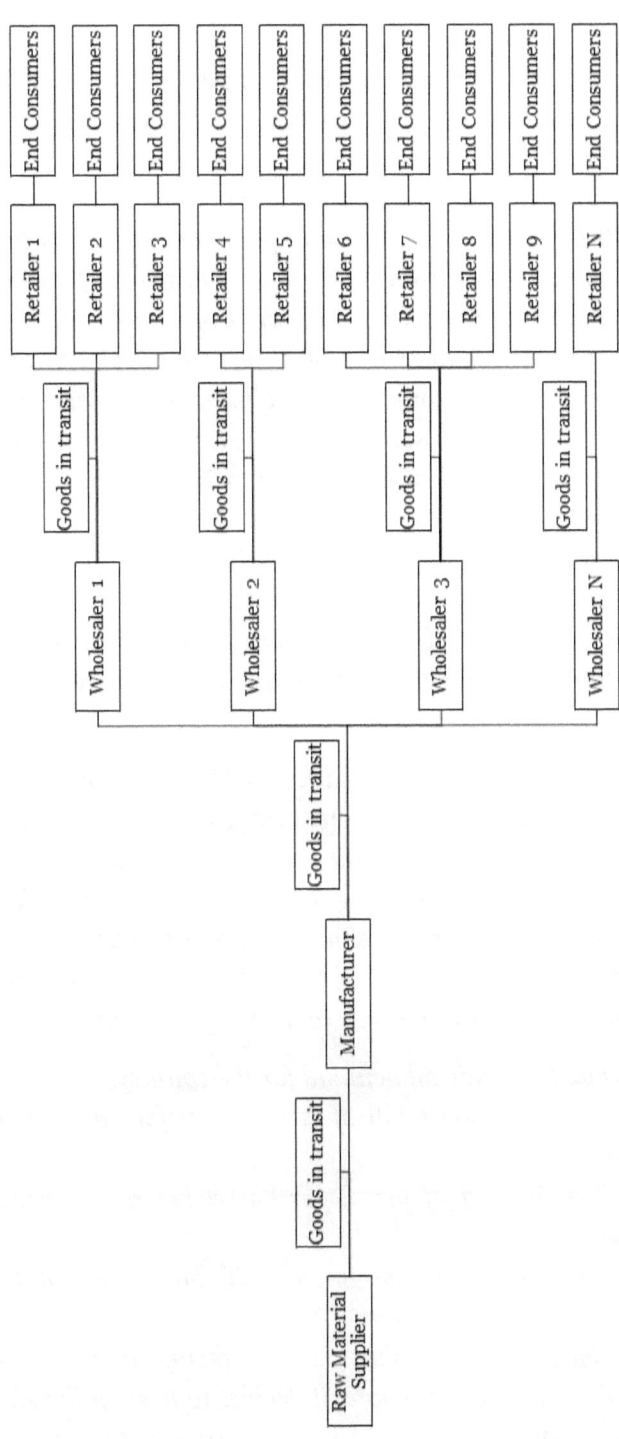

Quiz:

A country consumes one million barrels of petrol a day. It does not have any crude oil reserves. It is entirely dependent on crude oil imports for producing petrol. Typical voyage time for crude oil transport to reach the shores from a crude oil-exporting country is 10 days. The country maintains 20 days of crude oil at any point-in-time in its bunkers as a strategic reserve to mitigate any emergencies in the supply. The shipment containers remain in the port for three days before they are supplied to a refining industry. The country has only one refining plant, which satisfies the petrol demand for the country. The refining plant maintains a stock of three days of crude oil and seven days of petrol reserves in its possession. It refines the crude oil and supplies petrol to 10 states in the country. The demand for petrol in each state is almost the same. It is estimated that a day's petrol demand is in transit from the refining plant to the states. Each state distributor maintains seven days of petrol demand of the state as buffer stock. Each state distributor in turn supplies to 100 petrol filling stations. Each petrol filling station maintains two days of local petrol demand in its underground tank.

Assume, a barrel of crude oil produces 0.45 barrels of petrol. A barrel of crude oil costs $50. The shipment through seas costs $5 per barrel of crude oil. The refining of crude oil costs $10 per barrel. Transportation within the country and retailing costs $15 per barrel. The Federal Government levies $20 per barrel of crude oil as excise duty. Each State Government levies $2 per barrel of petrol as VAT. The exporting country decides to increase the cost of crude oil to $70 per barrel.

1. *Calculate the crude oil demand for the country.*
2. *Calculate the import bill of crude oil before the crude oil price increase.*
3. *Calculate the cost of petrol per barrel before the crude oil price increase.*
4. *Calculate the additional import bill burden when the price is increased to $70 per barrel.*
5. *The Federal Government is not facing any election in the immediate future. Therefore, it decides to pass on the entire burden to the people but does not want consumers to feel overburdened*

and at the same time, does not want to give a window of opportunity to opposition parties to oppose the petrol price hike. How will you price petrol to meet the above objectives? What will be the price of petrol per barrel as per your pricing strategy?

6. The Federal Government is facing an election in the immediate future. It can absorb $10 per barrel of crude oil and decides to pass on the burden of balance $10 per barrel of crude oil to consumers. What will be the price of petrol per barrel as per your pricing strategy?

7. The Federal Government expects the sale of automobiles to increase by 20% every year for the next five years and decides to augment its refining capacity, strategic reserves, and buffer stock. Estimate the crude oil demand in the fifth year assuming a unit proportional relationship between crude oil imports and automobile growth.

Understanding the Production Strategies for Marketing

Along with economics, production strategies also play a significant role in pricing strategies of products. Entities decide production strategies based on the demand forecast, cycle time, lead time, manufacturing capacities, supply network, distribution network, and warehousing facilities to optimize their production strategies.

Cycle time is the time taken for manufacturing products. This is also called as *production time.*

Lead time is the time taken from the date of order to the date of order fulfillment.

Make-to-Stock (MTS) is a production strategy where an entity manufactures goods based on future demand by adjusting its production. If the demand forecasting is inaccurate, this production strategy could lead to surplus or deficit stock. While deficit production leads to loss of business revenues, surplus production leads to storage cost, spoilage cost, wastage cost, and theft cost. This production strategy does not allow customization of goods at the consumer end. To address different consumer preferences, the manufacturer produces goods in various specifications and varieties. There is no lead time involved in MTS as goods are stocked on shelves of retail shops awaiting purchase.

Make-to-Order (MTO) is a production strategy where an entity manufactures goods for the actual demand. This production strategy is adopted when the lead time is less, and/or when the inventory storage cost is higher. If the lead time is longer, it can hurt the business turnover as an order is initiated on the demand and that consumers may not like to wait for long unless there is a strong brand loyalty quotient. This production strategy allows for mass customization of goods but not at order-level customization of goods.

Assemble-to-Order (ATO) is a variation of MTO where the cycle time is a bottleneck in the lead time. When cycle time cannot be reduced, goods are manufactured as several components and are kept ready for assembling to lower the lead time. Sometimes, entities ship broken-down parts to assemble in foreign countries. This strategy might help them in reducing the cost of transportation and/or storage. In ATO, there is no specification difference in components of goods. The assembly of components and shipment of goods happens once an order is placed.

Configure-to-Order (CTO) is a variation of ATO where an entity produces the same component in different specifications and gives an option to consumers to pick and choose components for assembling.

Engineer-to-Order (ETO) is a production strategy where an entity starts conceptualizing, designing, manufacturing, and assembling an order once an order is placed.

Quiz:

Identify the production strategies for the following:

1. *An entity manufacturing different kinds of toothpaste*
2. *An entity manufacturing mobile phones*
3. *An entity manufacturing cars*
4. *An iPhone assembled in India*
5. *Ordering a sandwich from subway*
6. *Ordering a fresh Domino's pizza*
7. *Buying paint of favorite color from a paint shop*
8. *Sale of Dell computers and laptops*
9. *Tailoring a dress of your size and liking*
10. *Manufacturing of boilers for a nuclear plant*

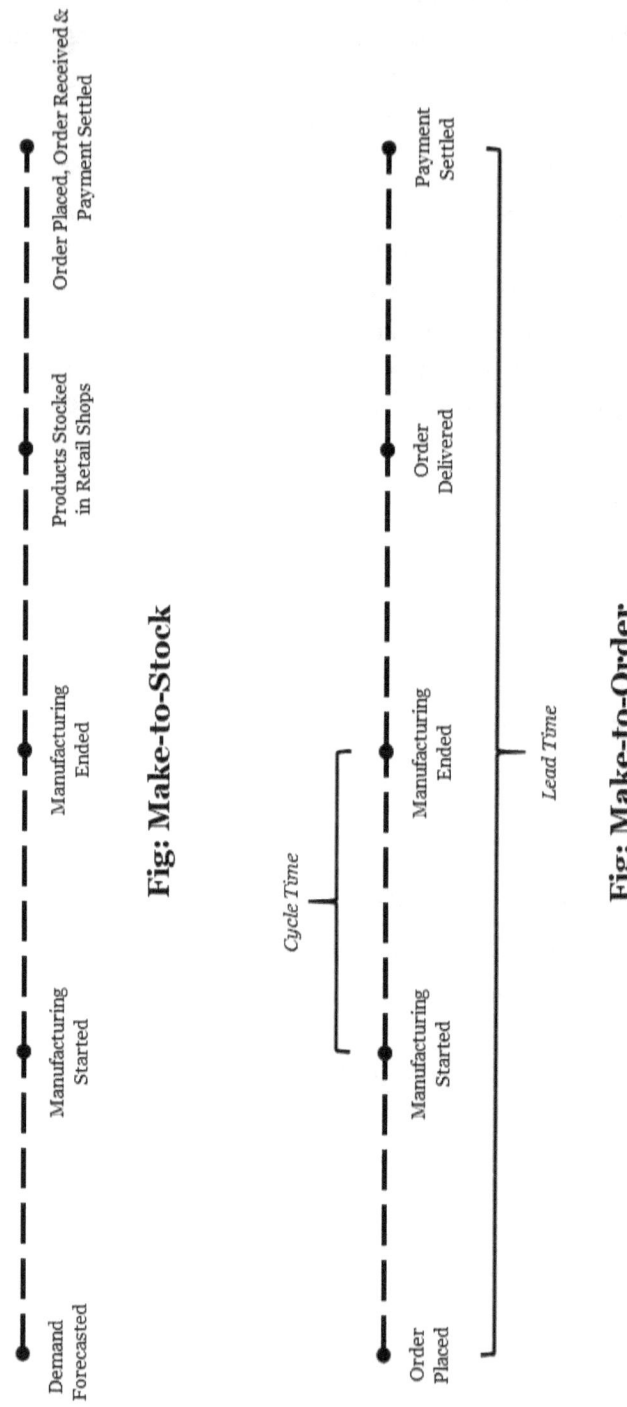

Fig: Make-to-Stock

Fig: Make-to-Order

Demand Forecasted — Parts Manufacturing Started (No Parts Variation) — Parts Manufacturing Ended — Order Placed — Parts Assembled — Order Delivered — Payment Settled

Fig: Assemble-to-Order

Demand Forecasted — Parts Manufacturing Started (With Parts Variation) — Parts Manufacturing Ended — Order Configured & Order Placed — Configured Parts Assembled — Order Delivered — Payment Settled

Fig: Configure-to-Order

Order Placed — Engineering Started — Engineering Ended — Manufacturing Started — Manufacturing Ended — Order Delivered — Payment Settled

Fig: Engineer-to-Order

Attributes of a Successful Marketer

In previous chapters, I have explained marketing concepts, frameworks, terminologies, mediums, strategies, and metrics. In this chapter, I highlight attributes that make a marketer successful in the profession.

I learned through my experiences and observed from my industry peers as well as colleagues that ten major qualities and skill sets define the success of a marketer. They are:

1. Understand the pulse of consumers and strategies of competitors
2. Explore new ideas, take informed risks, and make decisions
3. Think critically and analytically to solve problems
4. Display leadership and organizational ability
5. Be an active listener and have an eye-for-detail
6. Develop creativity, spontaneity, and aesthetics
7. Become a storyteller and content writer
8. Embrace technology
9. Keep learning vertically and horizontally
10. Never stick-on to your ego

In most organizations, decisions are top-down driven with no or little participation from the team. The top management disregards the fact that great ideas and solutions can originate from the people who are in direct communication with consumers and the market.

If the style of management functioning cannot be changed, the Head of Marketing can at least change the style of functioning within his/her department.

The Head of Marketing must display leadership skills and organizational ability to make the team participative and collaborative. The Head of Marketing must constantly evaluate products or services offering vis-à-vis that of competitors, new entrants and substitutes, external opportunities and threats with suitable marketing frameworks, understand the gap between products or services and the consumers' need/want, think critically and analytically about the consumers' problems to generate new ideas, develop solutions through new ideas, and make decisions after risk assessment.

In recent years, marketers are expected to be creative in marketing communication, spontaneous in generating promotional ideas, and artistic in designing marketing materials. Marketers are also expected to tell engaging stories through gripping content, embrace digital technologies and futuristic technologies to explore new marketing avenues and be effective on return-on-marketing investment.

In order to succeed as a marketer, one must also understand how production, inventory management, supply chain, economics, and consumer psychology play a part in marketing products or services to consumers.

To end this book with a parting statement – do not hesitate to kill products or services that are not giving traction to the business. Stay alive to the changing demand of consumers, stay alive to the competition, innovate new products or services, penetrate deeper into an existing market, look for opportunities to expand into new markets, explore relevant marketing avenues, experiment but measure success, and never compromise on the brand promise!